Westport Ontario and Area in Colour Photos, Saving Our History One Photo at a Time

Photography
by Barbara Raué
2016

Series Name:
Cruising Ontario

Book 161: Westport, Inverary,
Elginburg, Port Elmsley

Cover photo: 11 Church Street, Westport, Page 28

Series Name: Cruising Ontario
Saving Our History One Photo at a Time
in colour photos

Books Available in Alphabetical Order:
Aberfoyle, Acton, Alton, Amherstburg, Ancaster, Arthur, Aylmer, Ayr, Bloomingdale, Brantford, Burlington, Caledon, Caledonia, Cambridge, Clifford, Conestogo, Delhi, Dorchester to Aylmer, Drayton, Drumbo, Dundas, Eden Mills, Elmira, Elora, Essex, Fergus, Guelph, Hagersville, Hamilton, Hanover, Harriston, Hespeler, Jarvis, Kingston, Kingsville, Kitchener, Linwood, Listowel, London, Lucknow, Mono, Mount Forest, Neustadt, New Hamburg, Niagara-on-the-Lake, Oakville, Orangeville, Orillia, Owen Sound, Palmerston, Peterborough, Petrolia, Port Elgin, Preston, Rockwood, Sarnia, Seaforth, Sheffield, Shelburne, Simcoe, Southampton, St. Jacobs, St. Marys, St. Thomas, Stoney Creek, Stratford, Thamesford, Tillsonburg, Waterdown, Waterford, Waterloo, Welland, Wellesley, Windsor, Wingham, Woodstock

Other Books by Barbara Raue

Coins of Gold

Arrows, Indians and Love

The Life and Times of Barbara
Volume 1: Inventions That Have Enhanced My Life
Volume 2: Entertainment That I Have Enjoyed
Volume 3: East Coast Trips
Volume 4: Olympics Have Always Intrigued Me
Volume 5: Wonders of the World
Volume 6: Caribbean Cruises We Have Enjoyed
Volume 7: Animals
Volume 8: Storms and Other Major Disasters in My Lifetime
Volume 9: Wars, Terrorist Attacks and Major Disasters

The Cromwell Family Book

Laura Secord Discovered

Daddy Where Are You?

Montana Series
Book 1: Montana Dream
Book 2: Life on the Montana Frontier
Book 3: Montana to Boston and Back

Visit Barbara's website to view all of her books
http://barbararaue.ca

Table of Contents

  Sawmills built by Sheldon Stoddard and the Manhard brothers in 1828-32, during the construction of the Rideau Canal, fostered the development of Westport. Grist mills and wharves were soon erected and by 1848 a post office was established. Within a decade the hamlet had three hundred residents and several prosperous businesses, including the General Store of Declan Foley and mills of William H. Fredenburgh, a prominent lumber exporter. The community's growth was stimulated by agricultural prosperity and the construction of the Brockville, Westport and Sault Ste. Marie Railway, completed in 1888 between Brockville and Westport, a distance of forty-five miles. With several takeovers, the railway continued to run until 1952.

  Inverary is a community in South Frontenac, Ontario. In 1845 it was called Storrington; in 1860 the name was changed to Inverary.

  Elginburg is located on Sydenham Road, County Road 9, in the County of Frontenac.

  Port Elmsley is located in eastern Ontario in Lanark County on the north shore of the Rideau River between the town of Perth and the town of Smiths Falls.

Westport

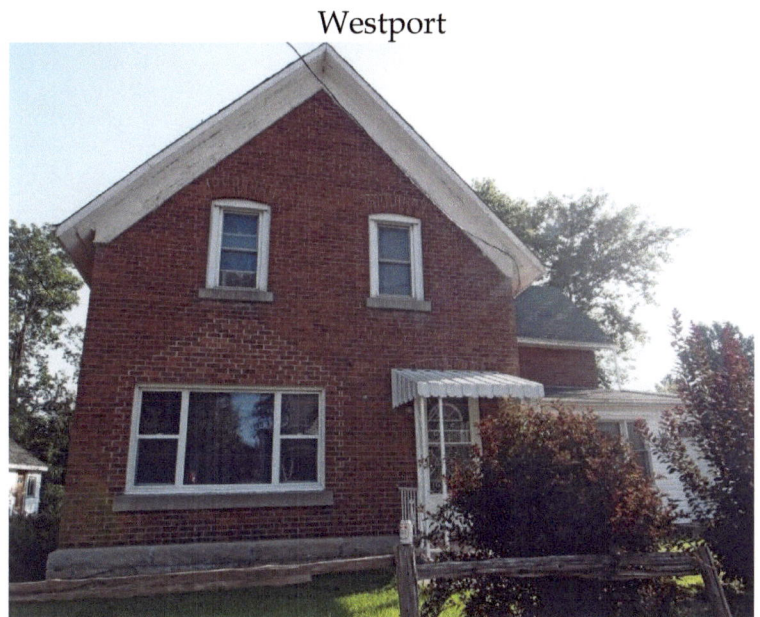

Gothic

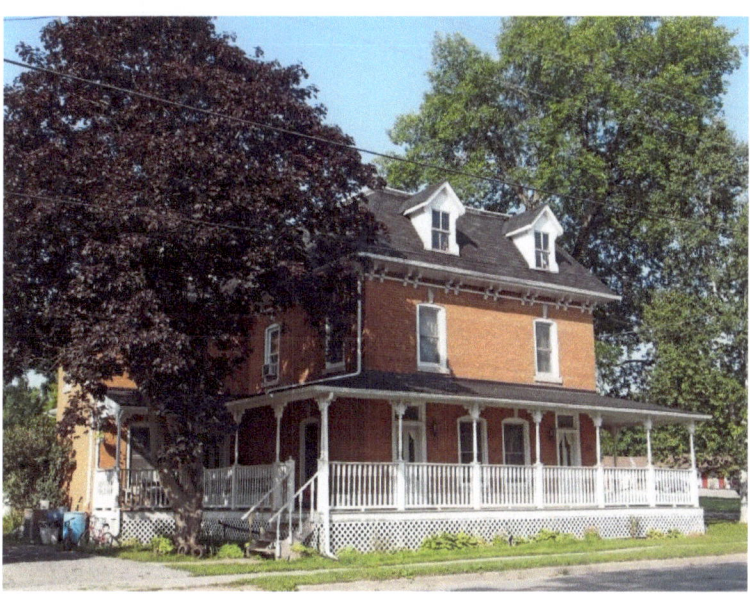

#56 - Second Empire – mansard roof, dormers, veranda pillars with decorative capitals, open railing, cornice brackets, voussoirs and keystones, transom windows

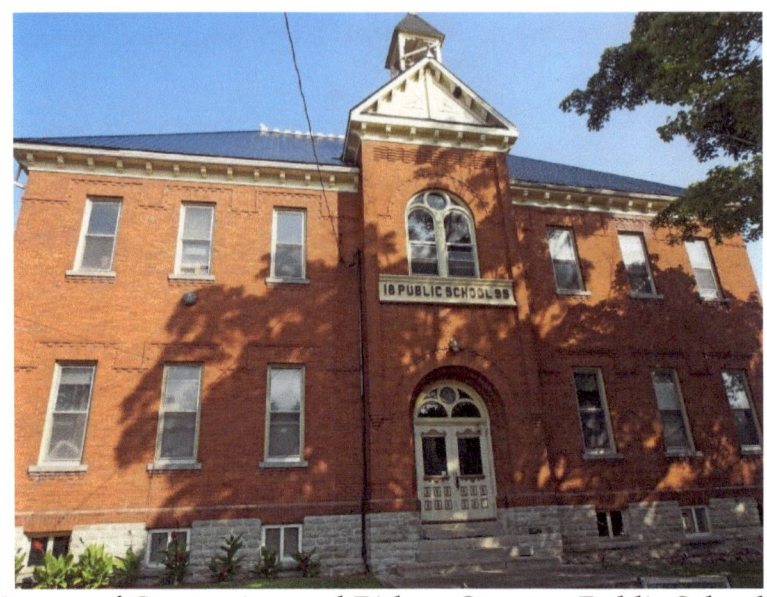

Corner of Concession and Rideau Streets - Public School –
1899 – frontispiece topped by pediment and bell cupola;
corbelling; cornice brackets, decorative brickwork

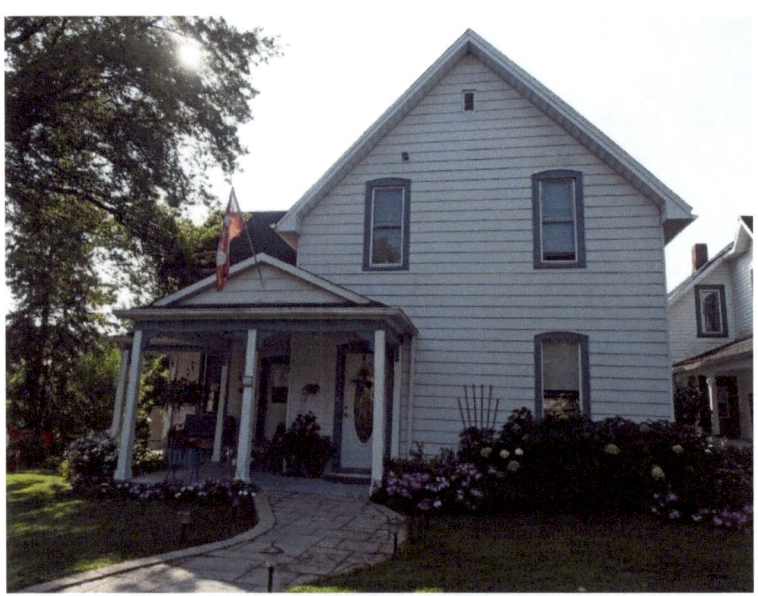

#25 - Gothic - pediment

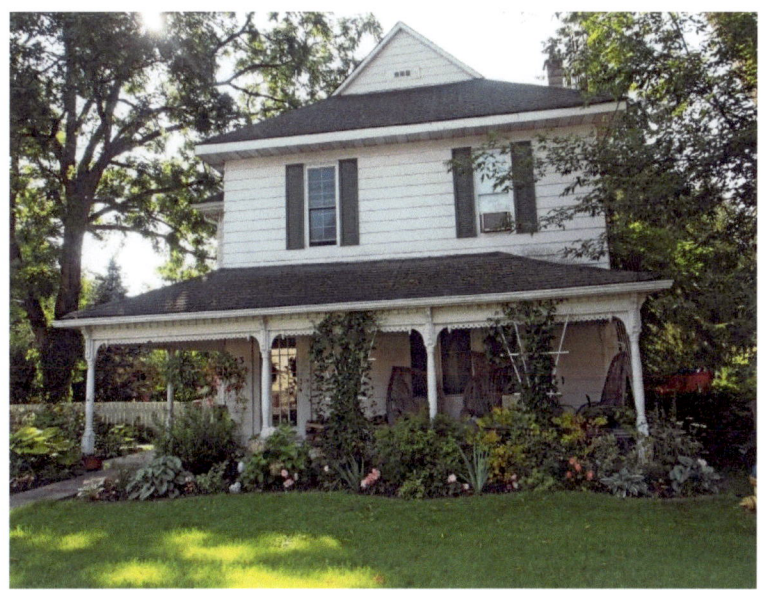

#23 – hipped roof with decorative pediment, decorative veranda spindles and capitals and bric-a-brac

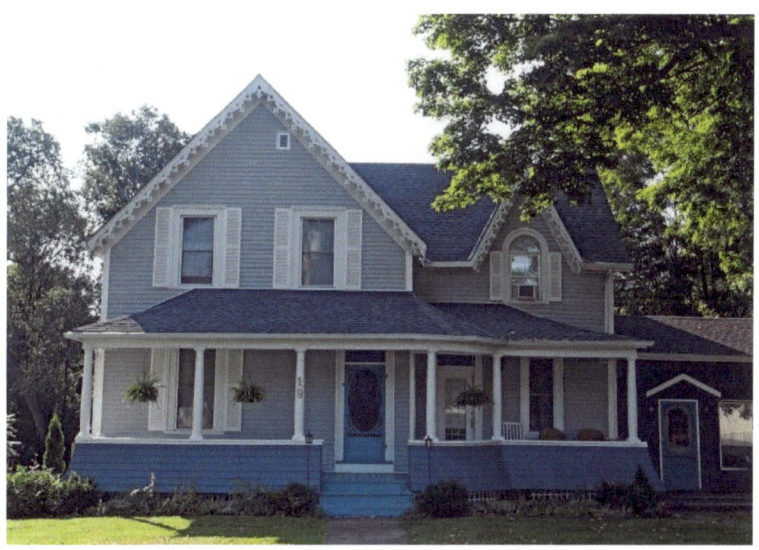

#19 - Victorian – verge board trim on gables, round-topped window in smaller gable

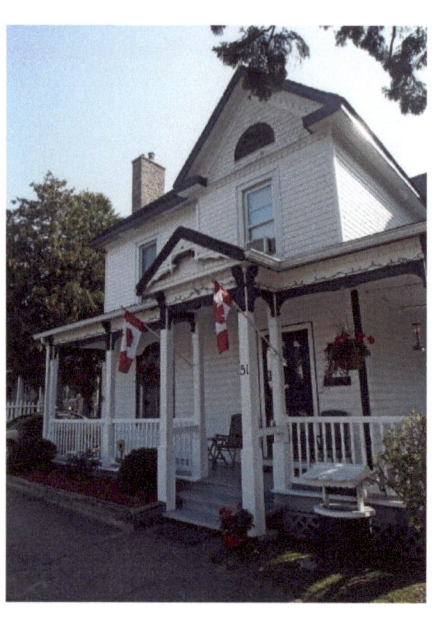

#51 – hipped roof, frontispiece with cornice return on upper gables, verge board trim on verandah pediment, decorative capitals on verandah posts

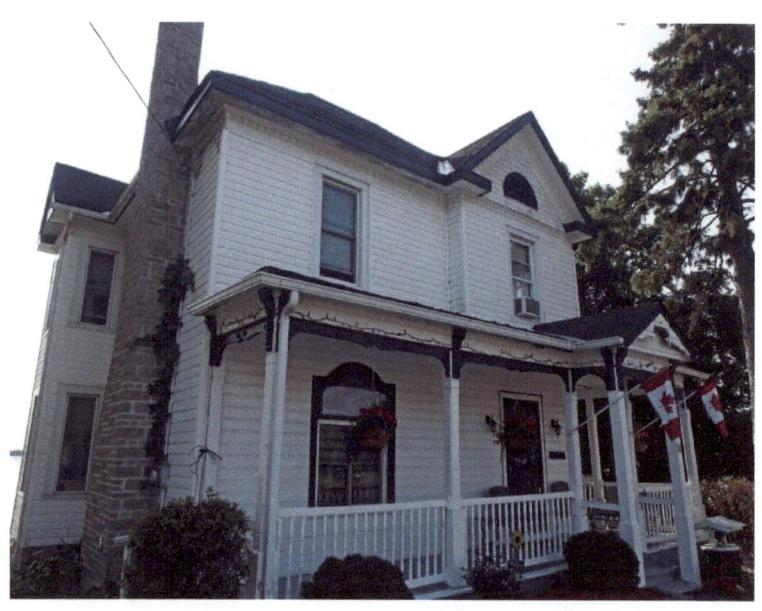

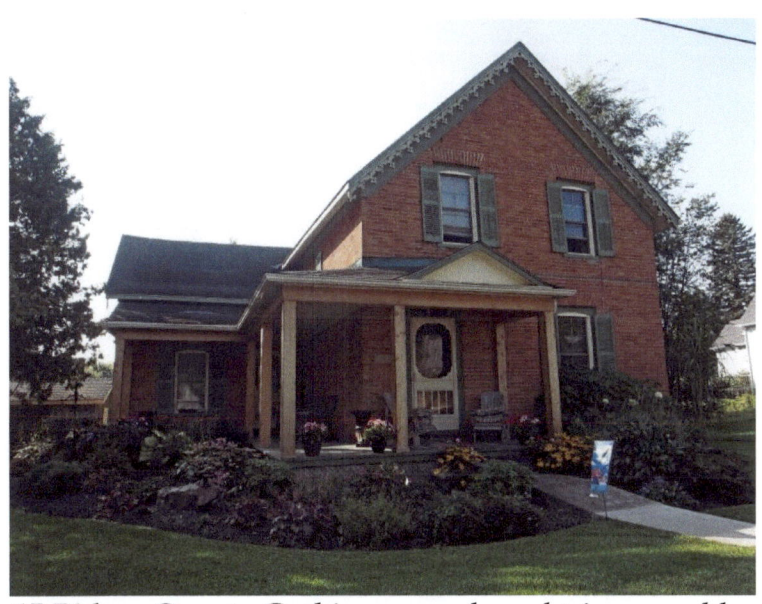

15 Rideau Street - Gothic – verge board trim on gable,
pediment

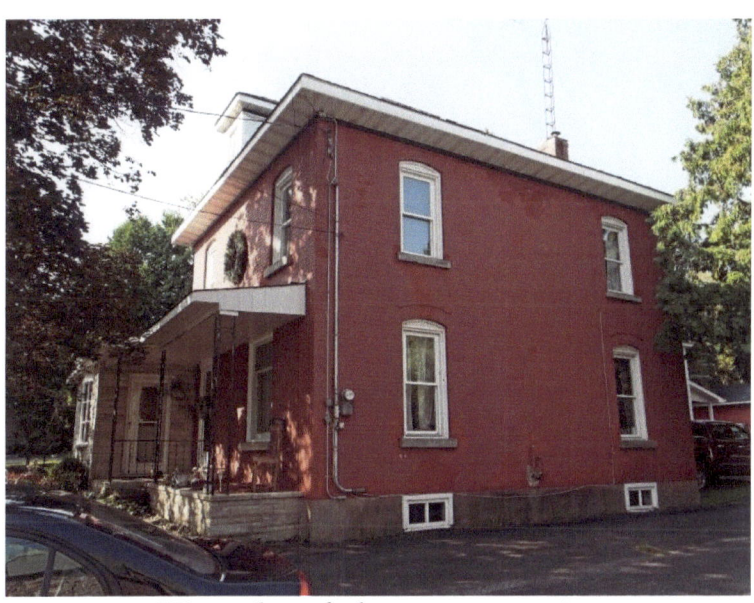

Hipped roof, dormer, voussoirs

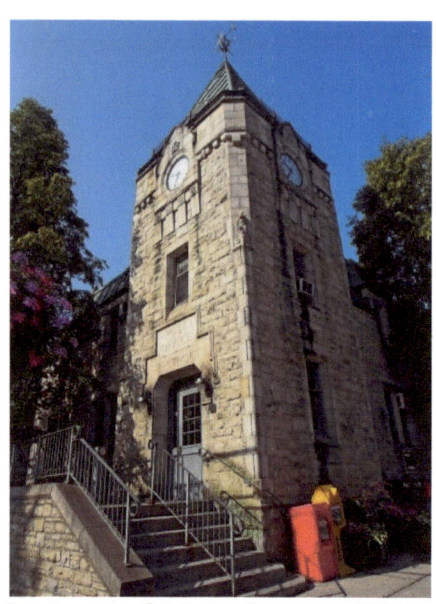

#36 - corner of Spring and Main Streets - Westport Post Office – built from local stone in 1935 – Chateau style – stone carvings of animals on the tower and around the door

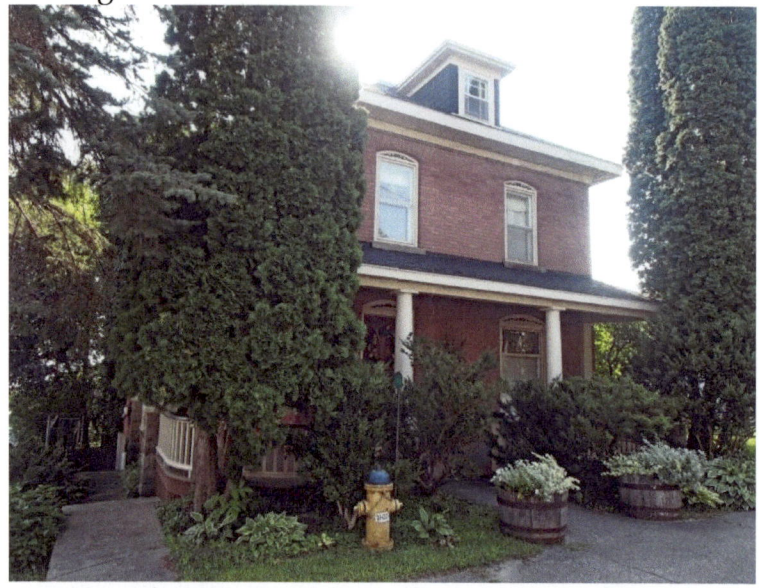

Hipped roof, dormer, Doric pillars, stained glass window

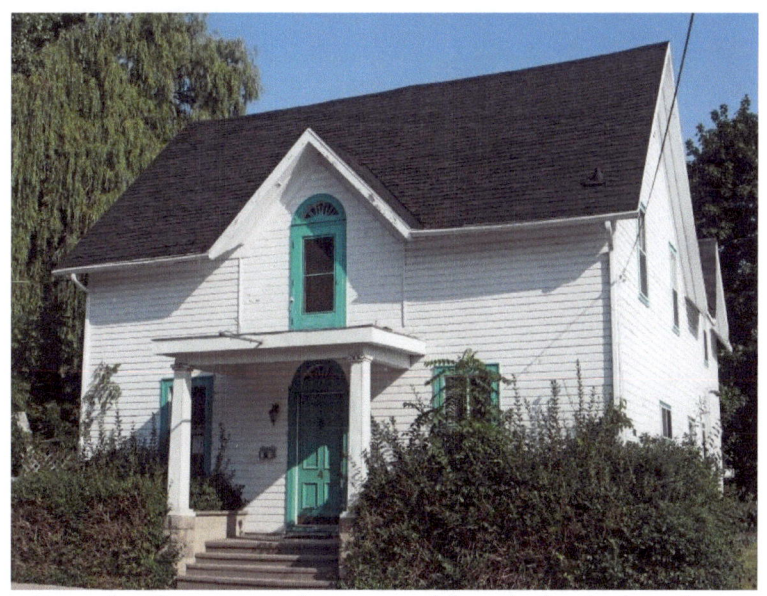

#4 - Ontario Cottage style – round-headed window in center gable

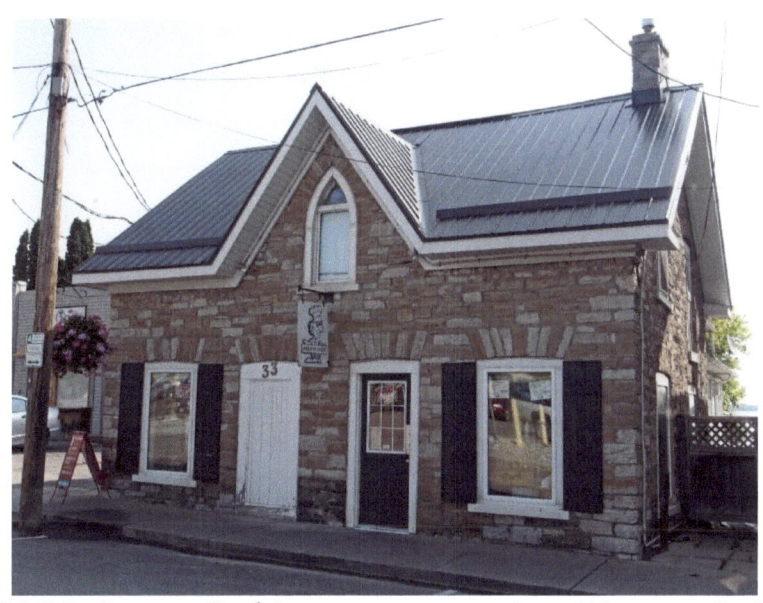

33 Main Street - Gothic – stone, voussoirs – Westport Swiss Bakery – bread and treats

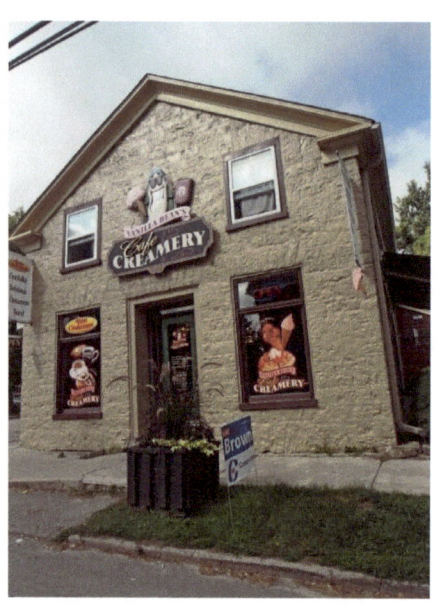

Cornice return on gable

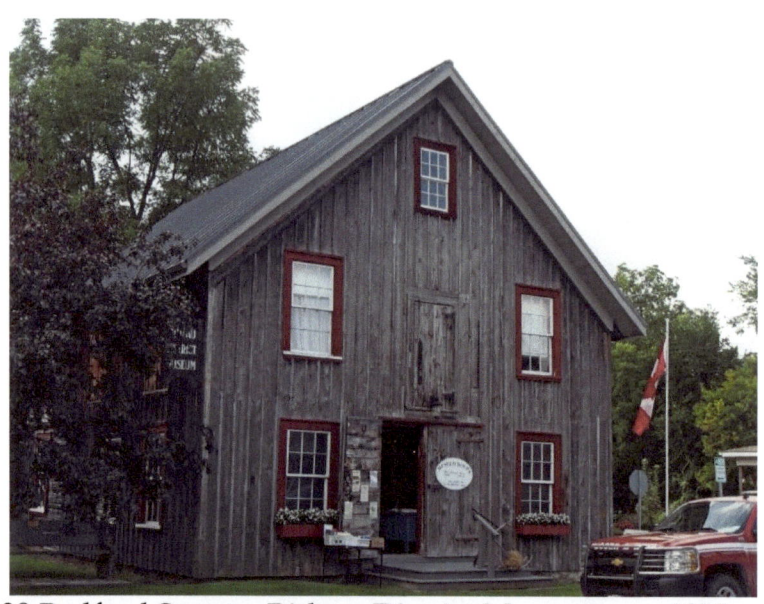

29 Bedford Street – Rideau District Museum – c. 1850s –
museum opened in the old blacksmith shop in 1961

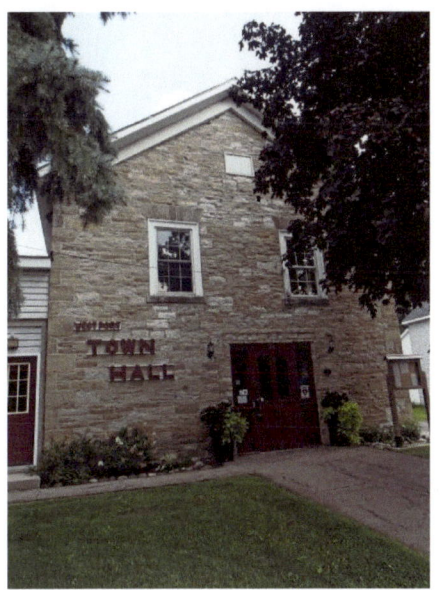

30 Bedford Street – Town Hall - 1853

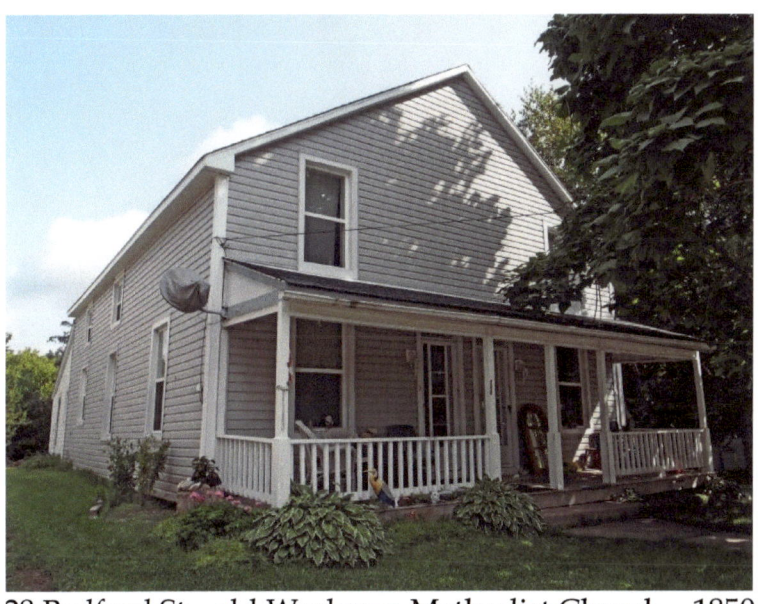

28 Bedford St - old Wesleyan Methodist Church – 1850

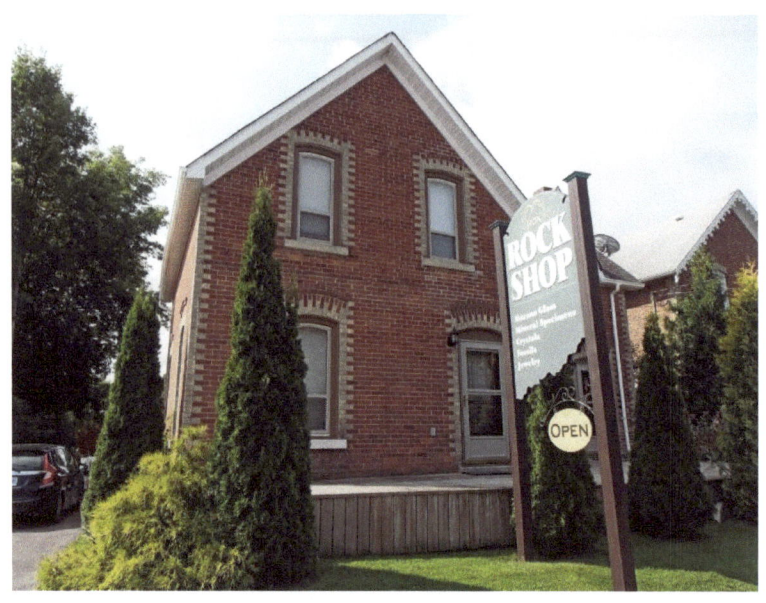

25 Bedford Street – Victorian – dichromatic brickwork, corner quoins

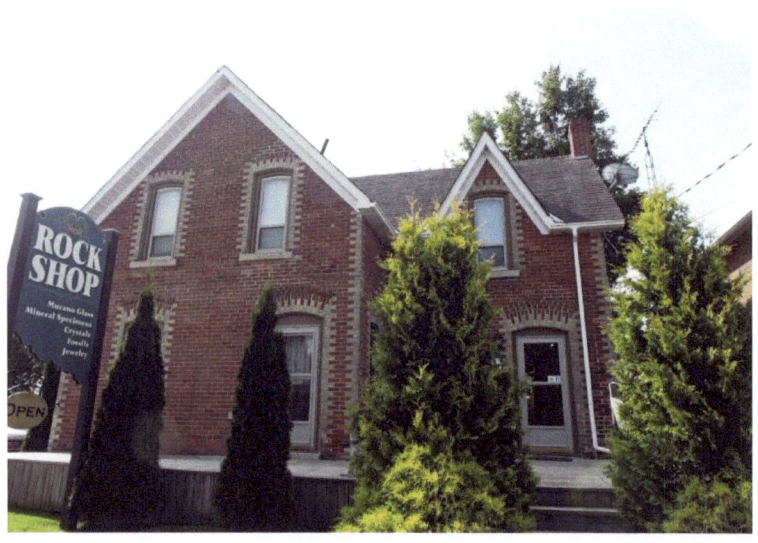

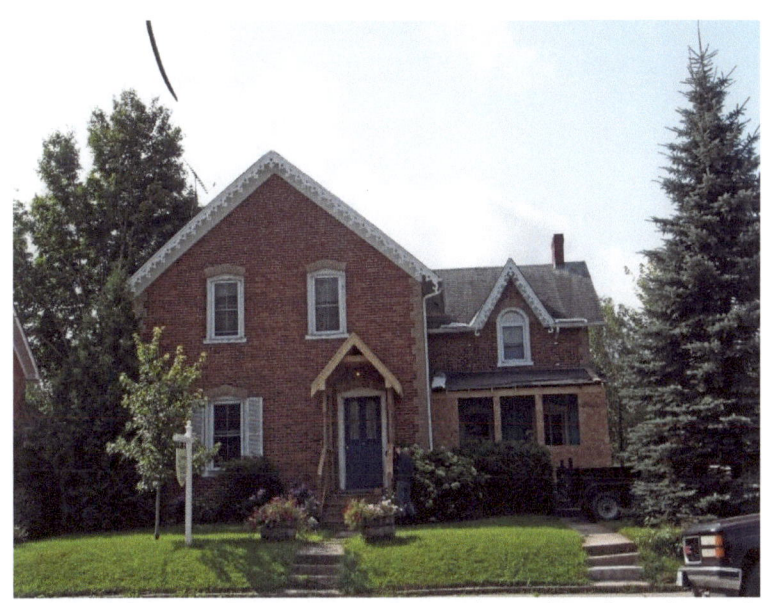

27 Bedford Street - Victorian - Gingerbread Bed and Breakfast
– gingerbread trim on gables, corner quoins

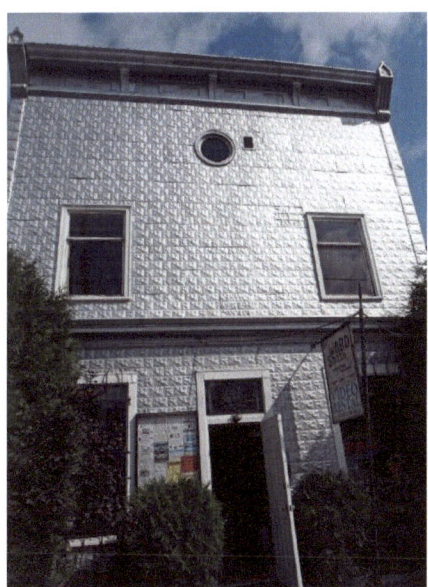

22 Bedford Street
– The Wordsmith

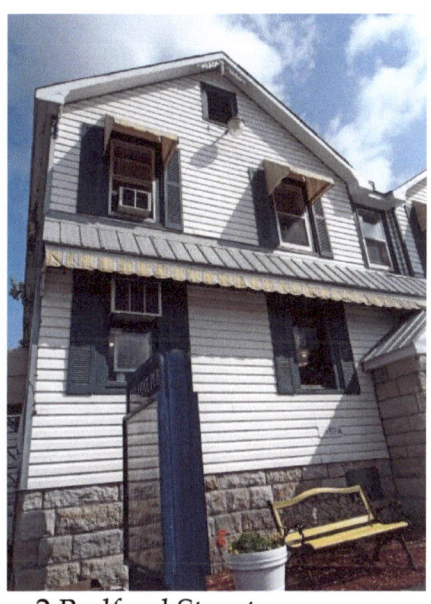

2 Bedford Street
The Cove Pub

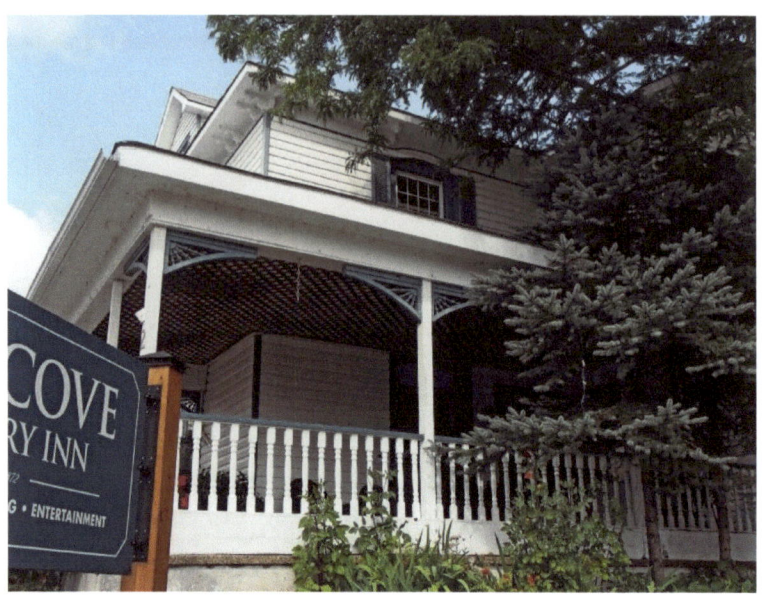

2 Bedford Street - W. H. Fredenburgh House – early merchant
and lumberman – c. 1876 – now The Cove Country Inn

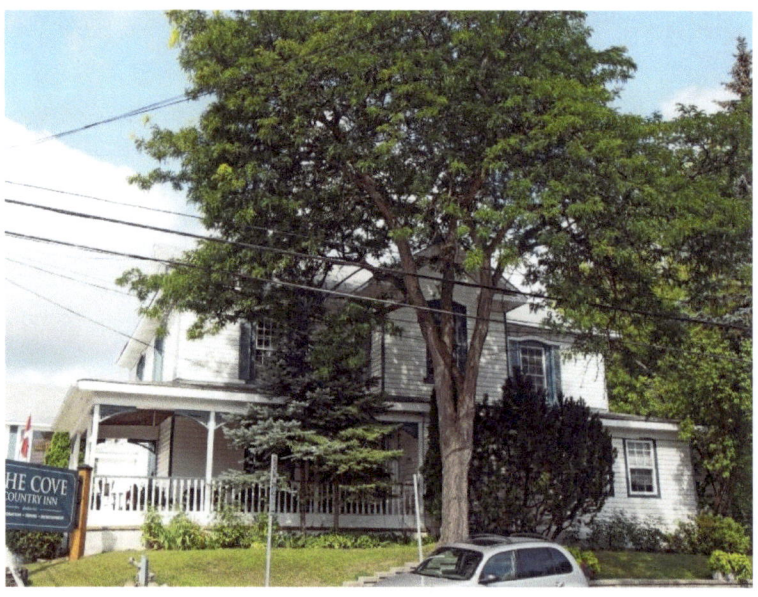

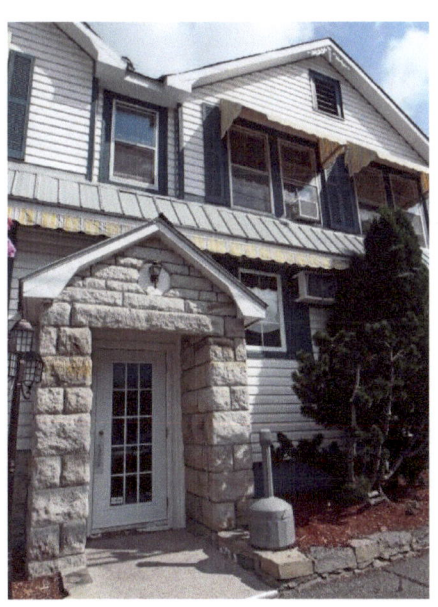

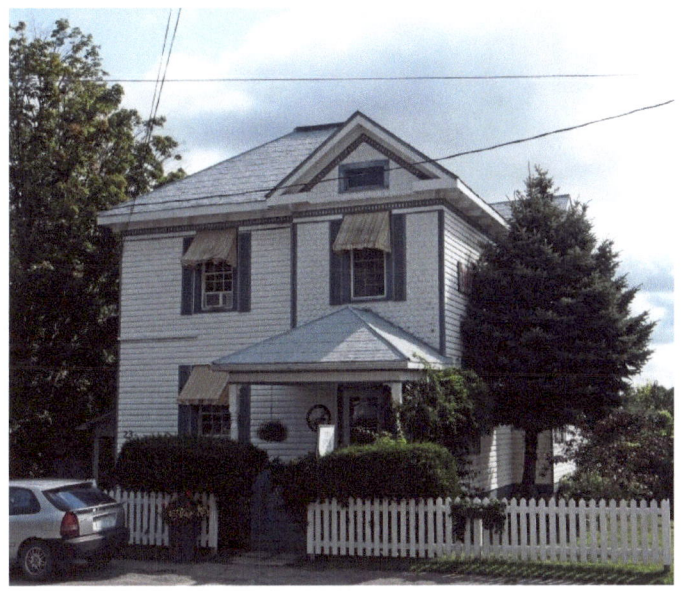

The Cove Country Inn

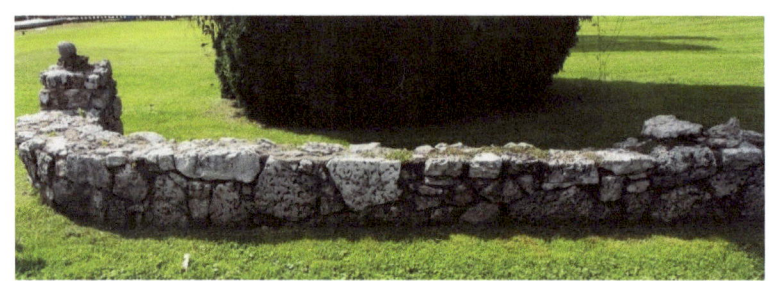

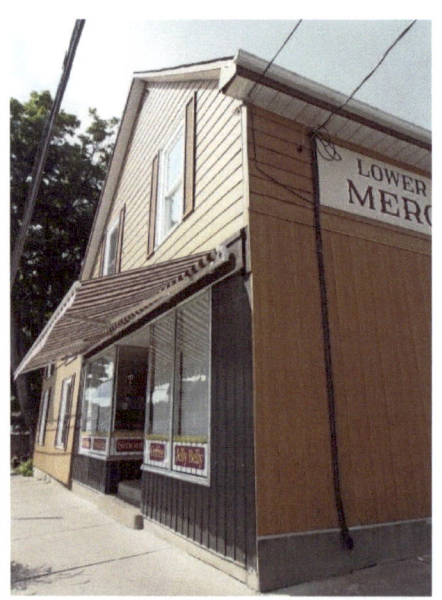

20 Main Street – Hiram W. Lockwood built a general store on the corner of Bedford and Main Streets in 1872. It is now the Lower Mountain Mercantile.

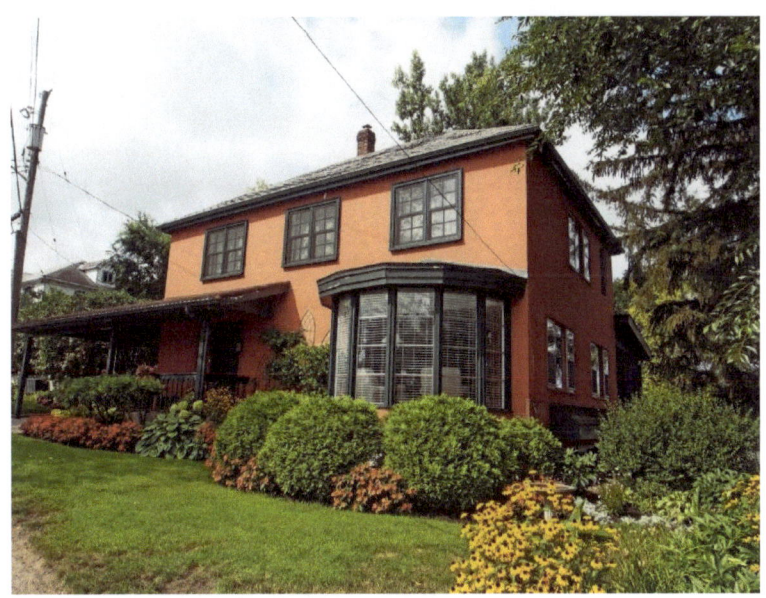

#18 - Hip roof, bay window

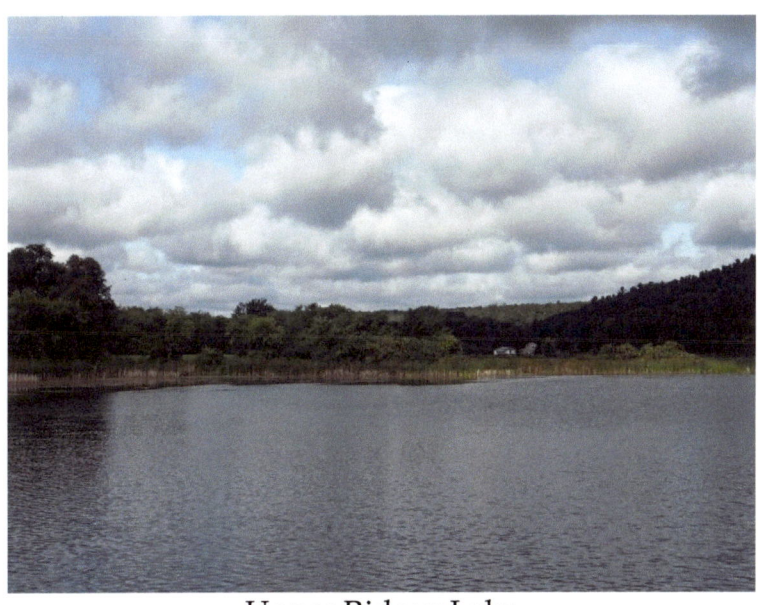

Upper Rideau Lake

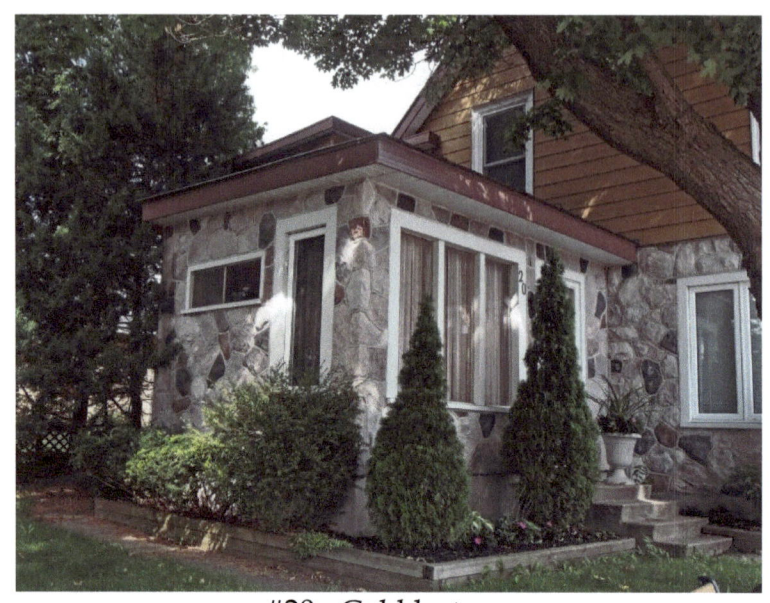

#20 - Cobblestone

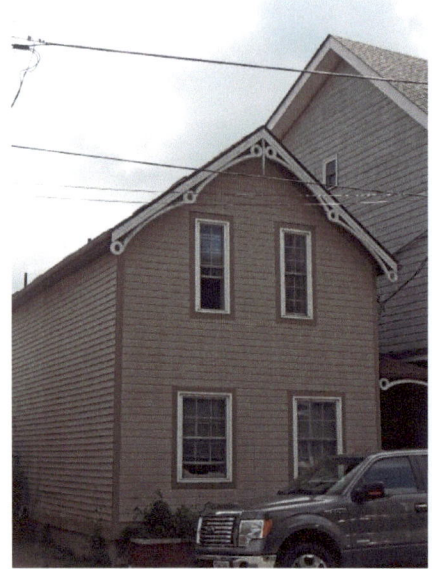

#41Main Street
Verge board trim on gable

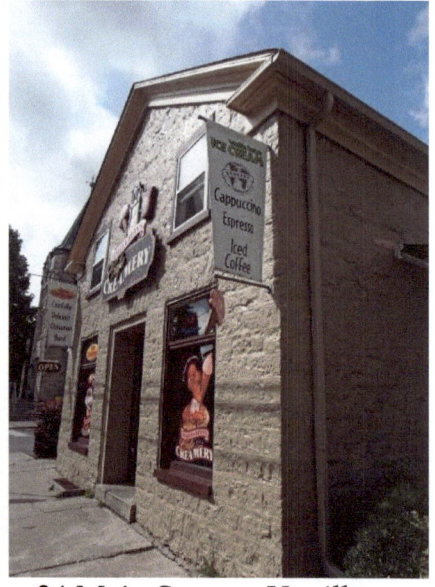

34 Main Street – Vanilla
Beans Café and Creamery -
cornice return on gable

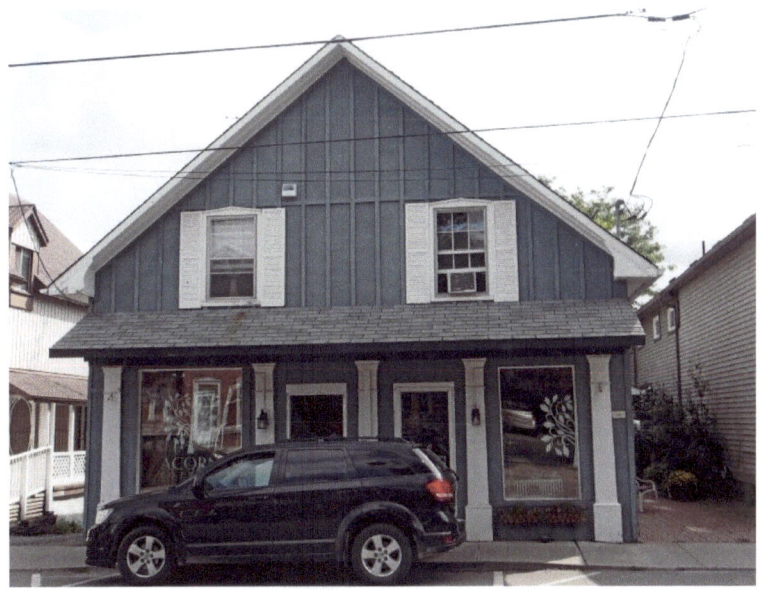

39 Main Street – Acorn Pottery

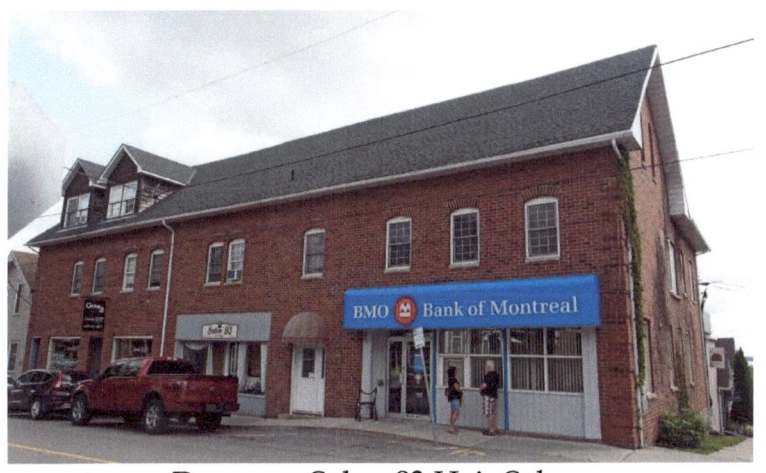

Dormers; Salon 93 Hair Salon;
41 Main Street East – BMO Bank of Montreal;
2 Spring Street - The Rustic Oven

Fetch Murphy Walk

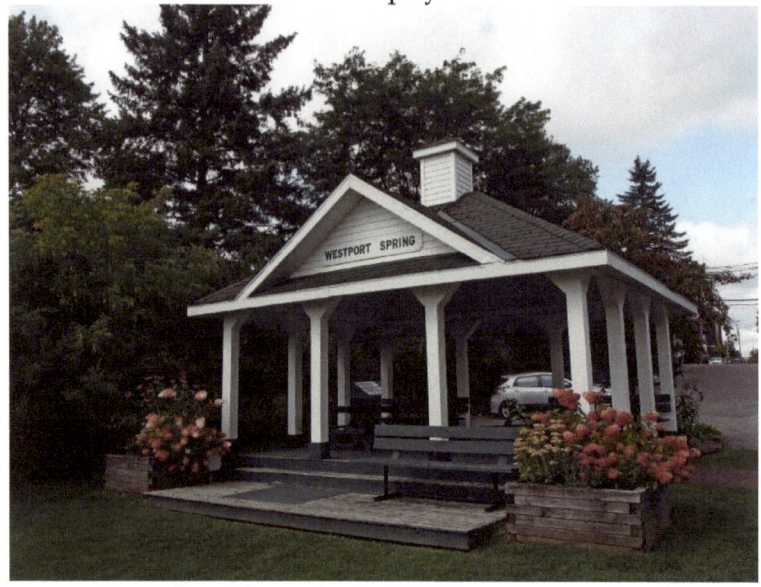

Indian artifacts found on this site indicate that it was used as a campsite. From pioneer days, it has been a focal point of the village.

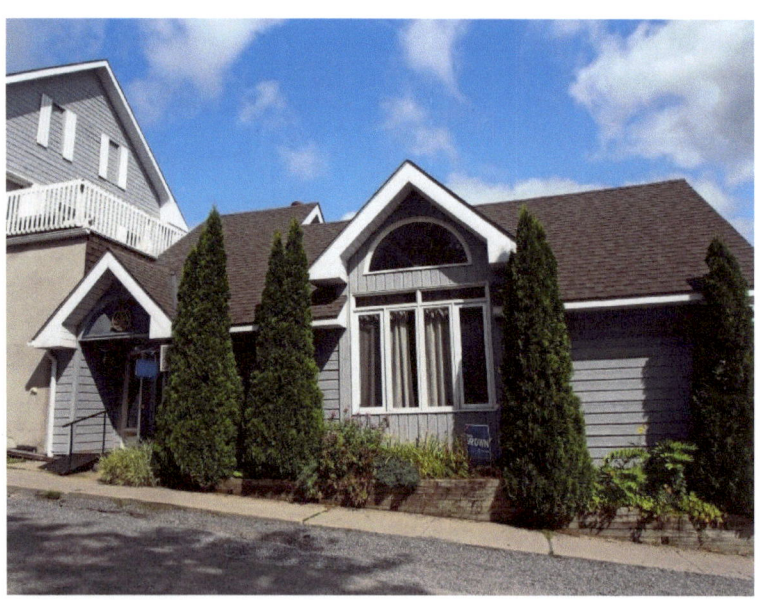

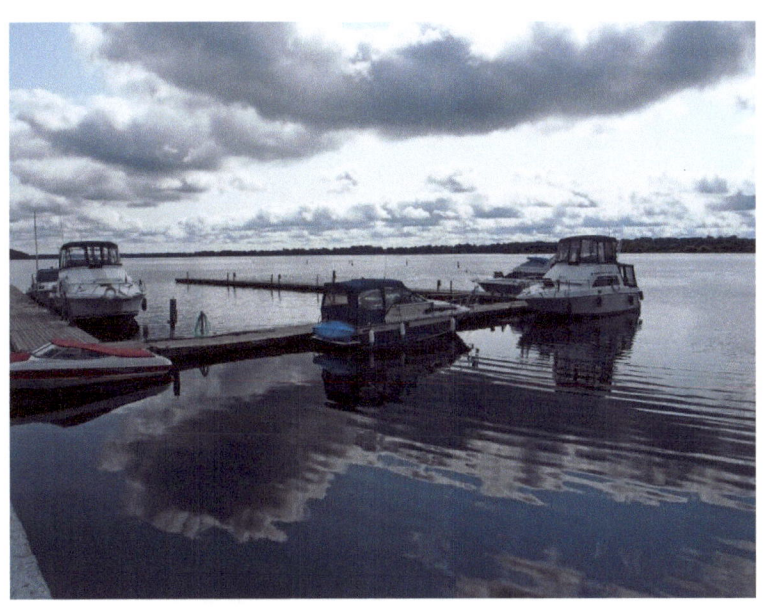

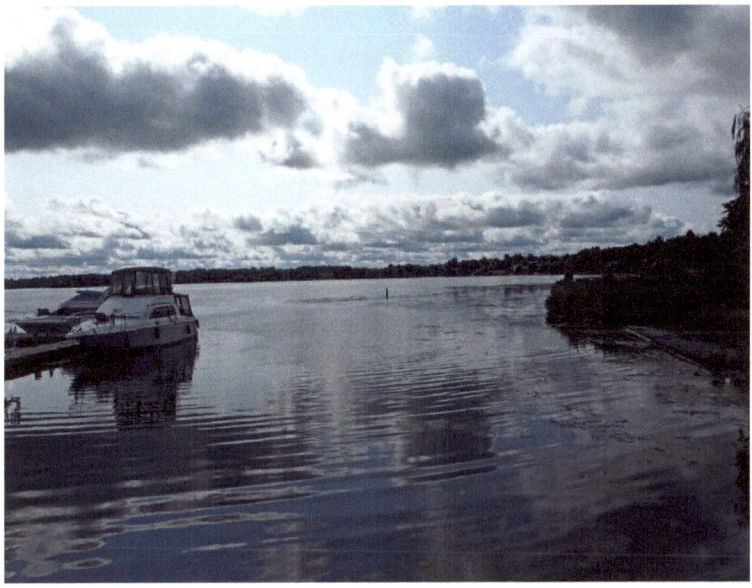

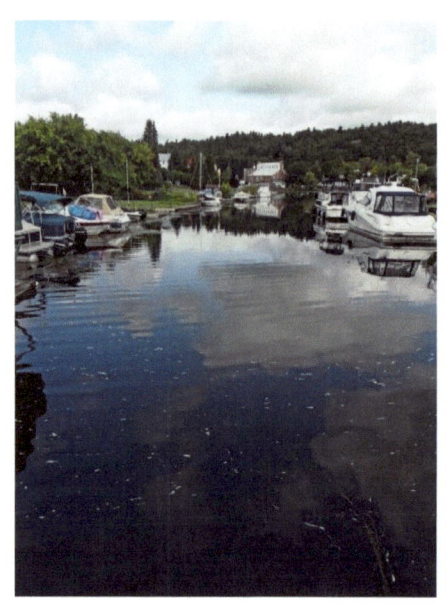

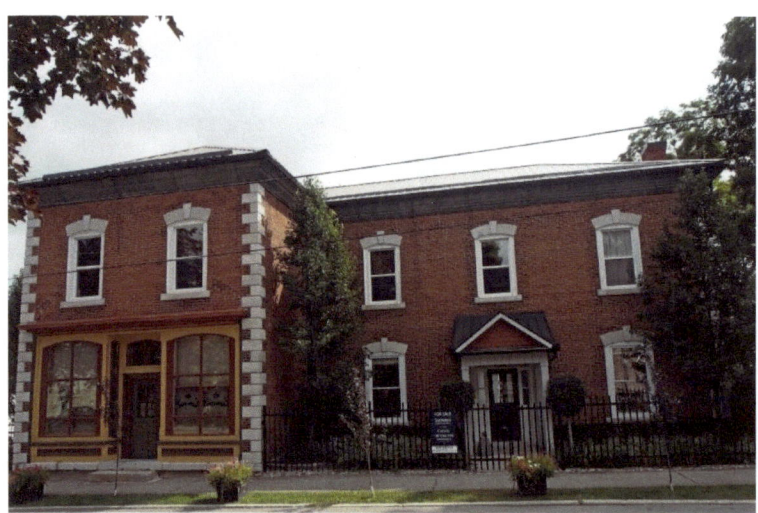

45 Main Street - The Prospector's Wife – corner quoins

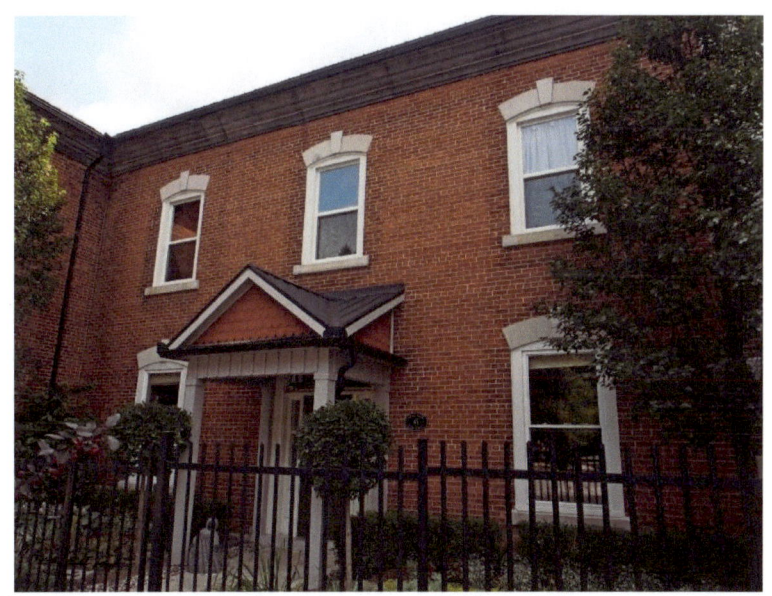

45 Main Street – Foley House - Declan Foley, a prominent businessman built a store and residence in 1864

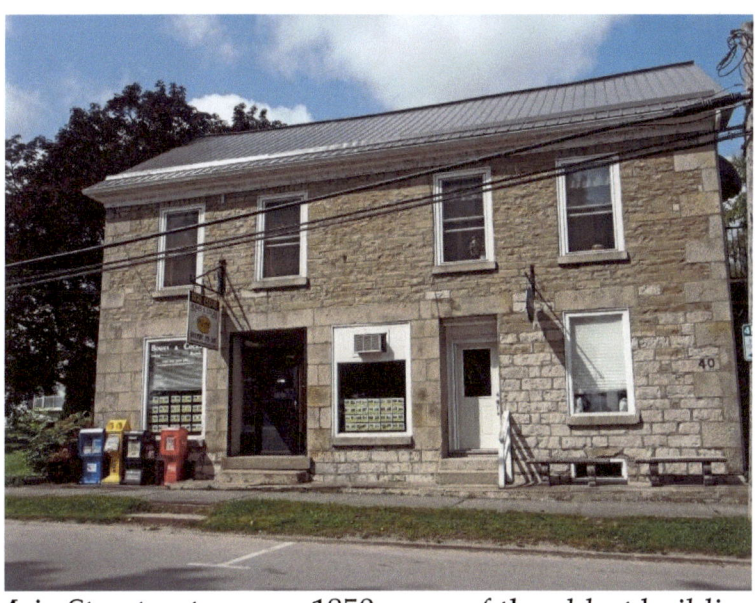

40 Main Street – stone – c. 1850 – one of the oldest buildings in Westport; corner quoins – at one time American House Hotel

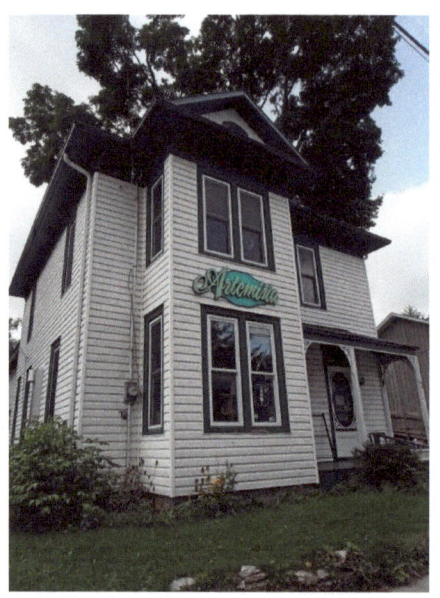
7 Spring Street - Artemisia

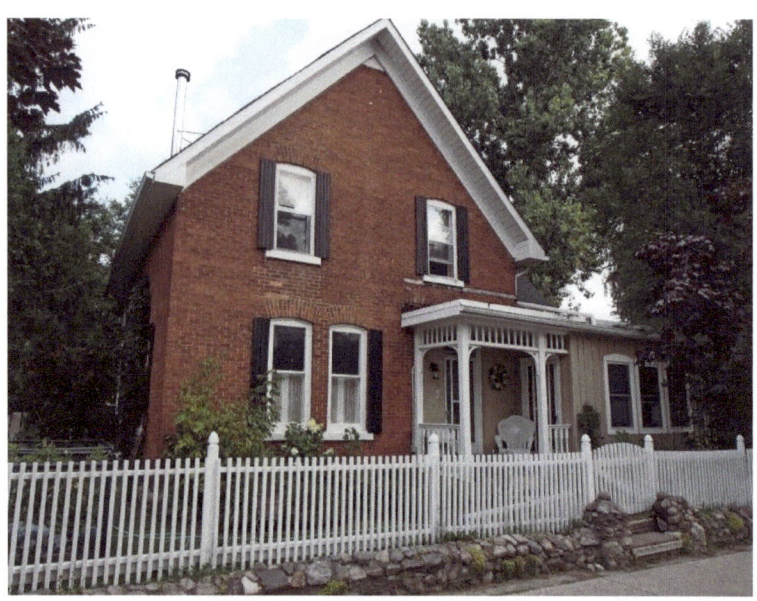
6 Spring Street - Gothic

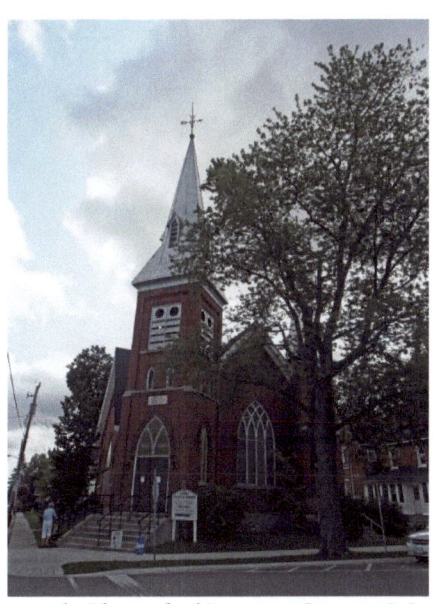

Spring Street United Church (Spring Street Methodist Church)
A.D. 1889 – three doorways, two spires; foundation is local
stone

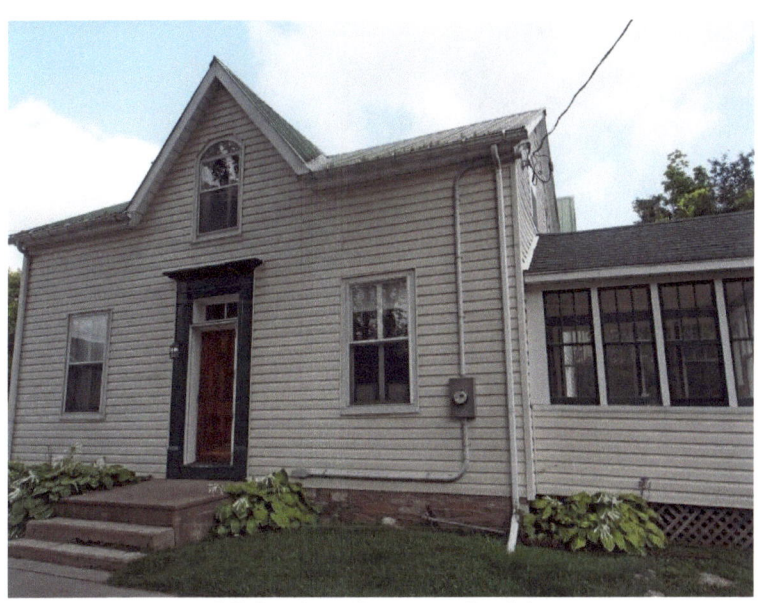

25 Spring Street - Gothic

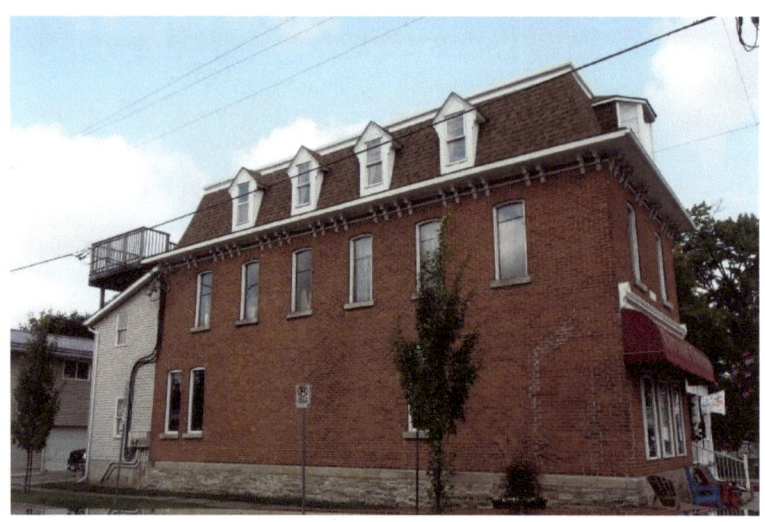

18 Church Street – built late 1880s as the home and shop of A.M. Craig, inventor of the one-piece harness buckle; Catholic Women's League Hall from 1921 to 1988; now Cottage Country – mansard roof with dormers

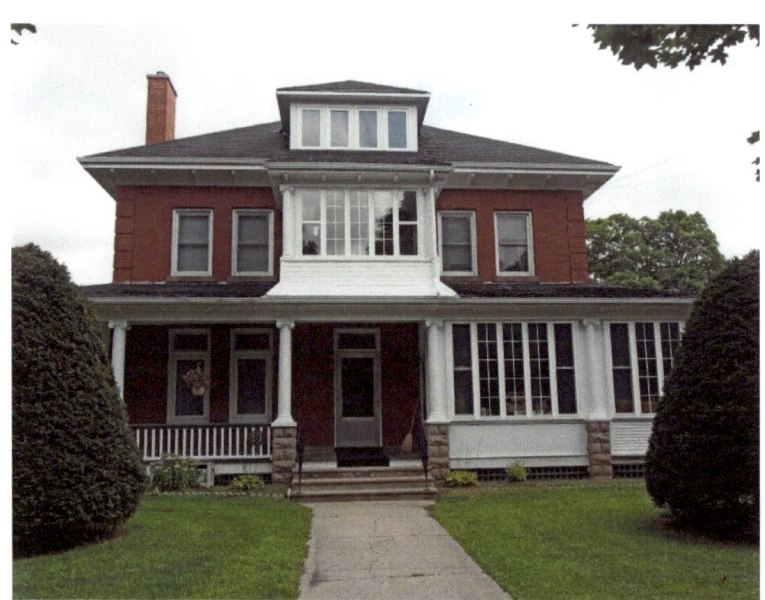

11 Church Street - Italianate style - hip roof, dormer, Ionic capitals on verandah pillars

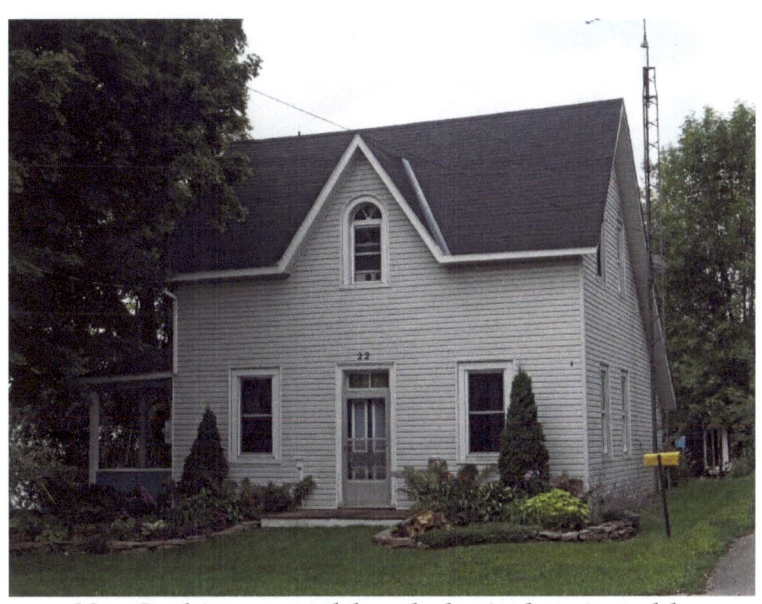

22 – Gothic – round-headed window in gable

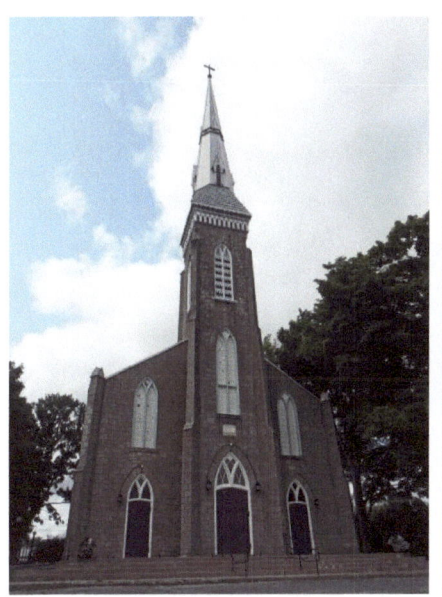
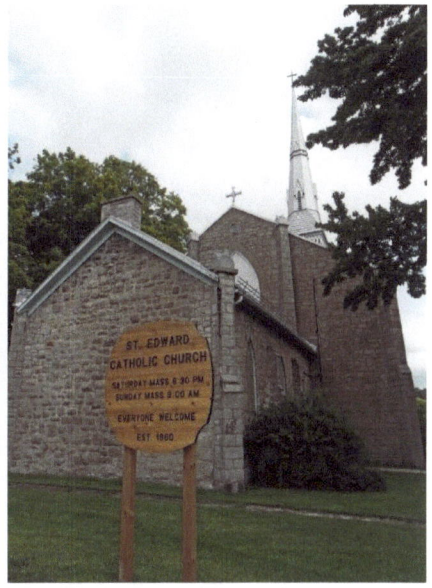

11 Concession Street - St. Edward's Catholic Church
Gothic Revival – lancet windows, buttresses

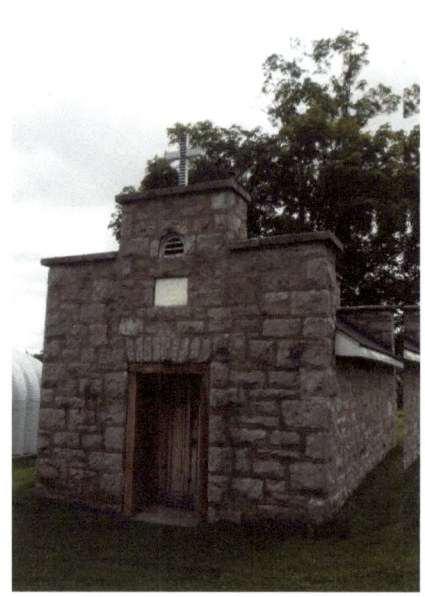

St. Edward's Parish vault

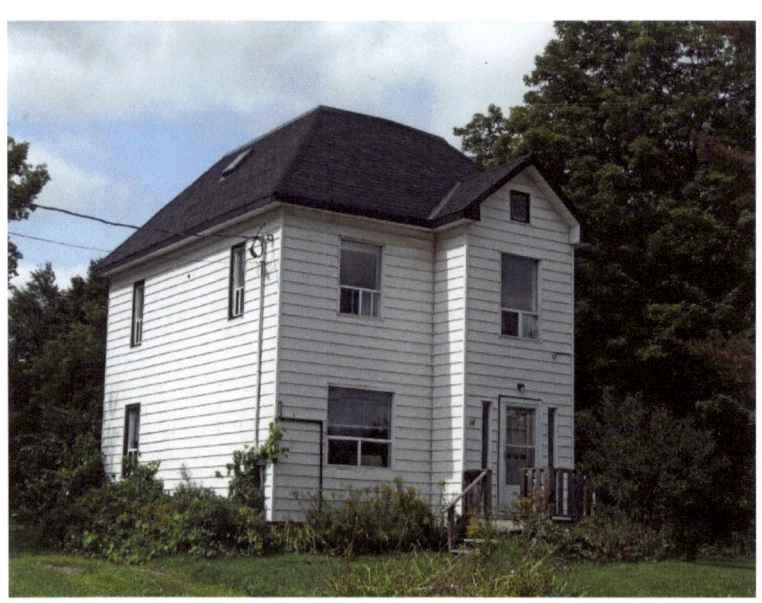

Hip roof, frontispiece

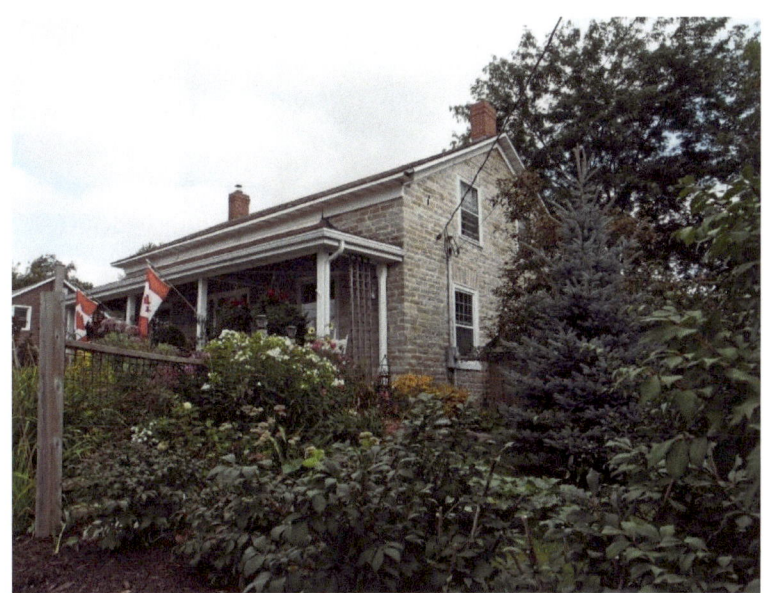

#4

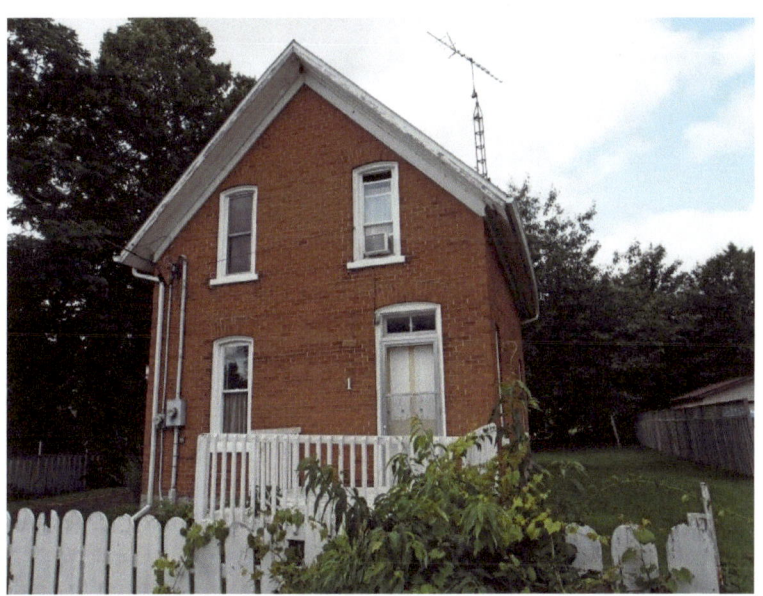

#1

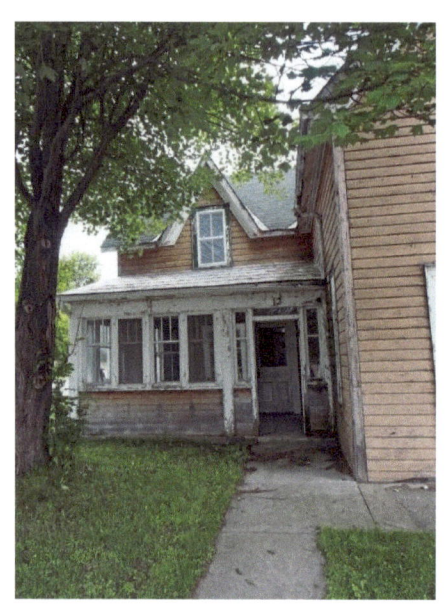

#12

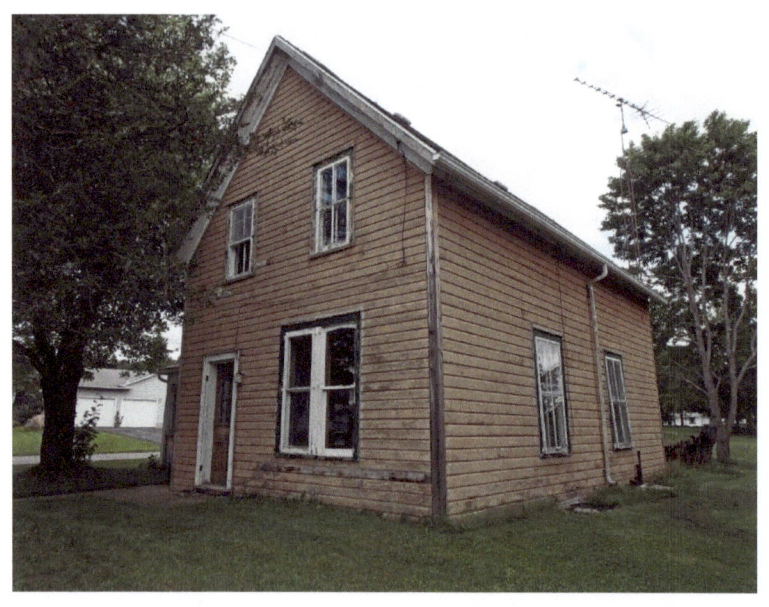

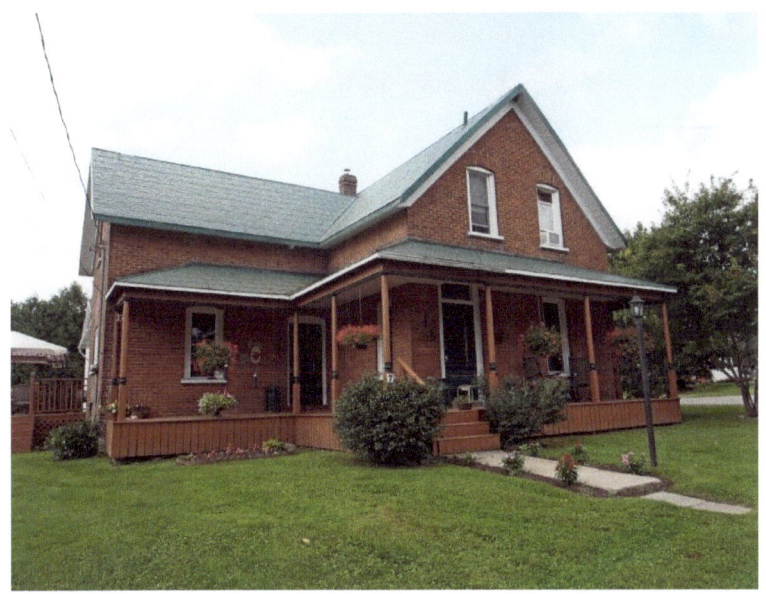

#7

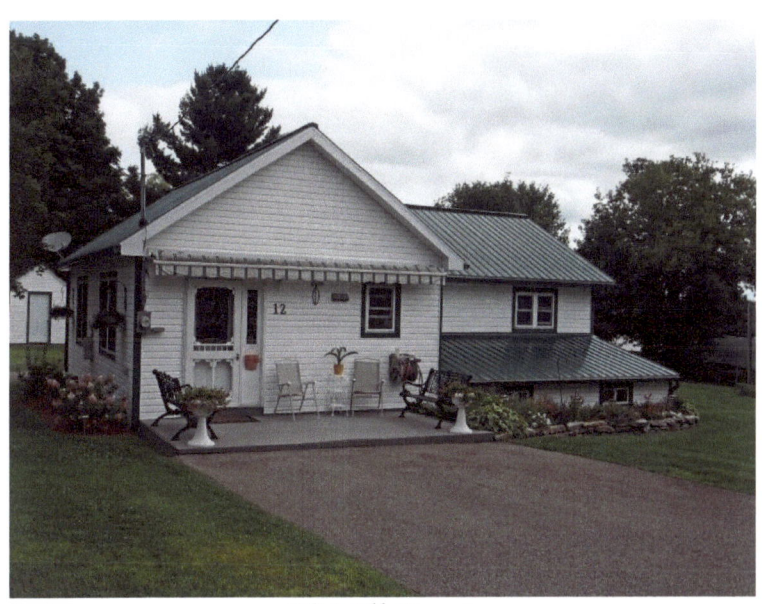

12 Mill Street

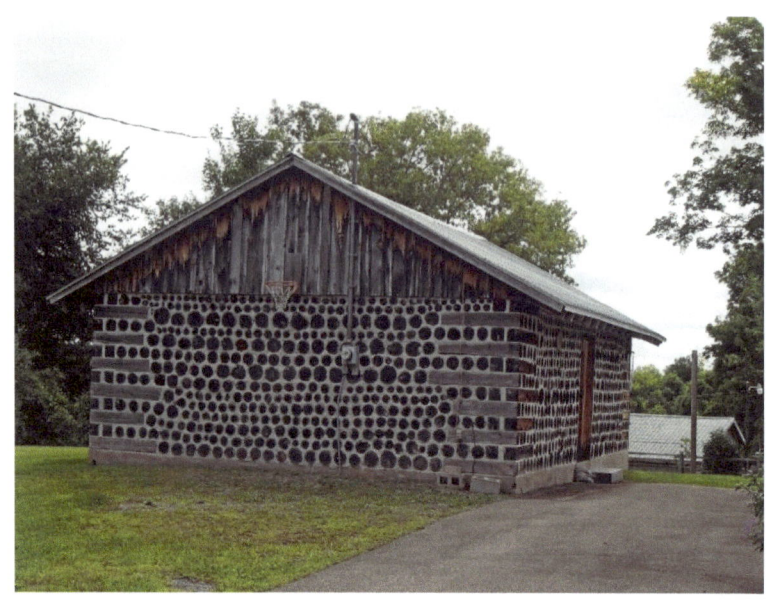

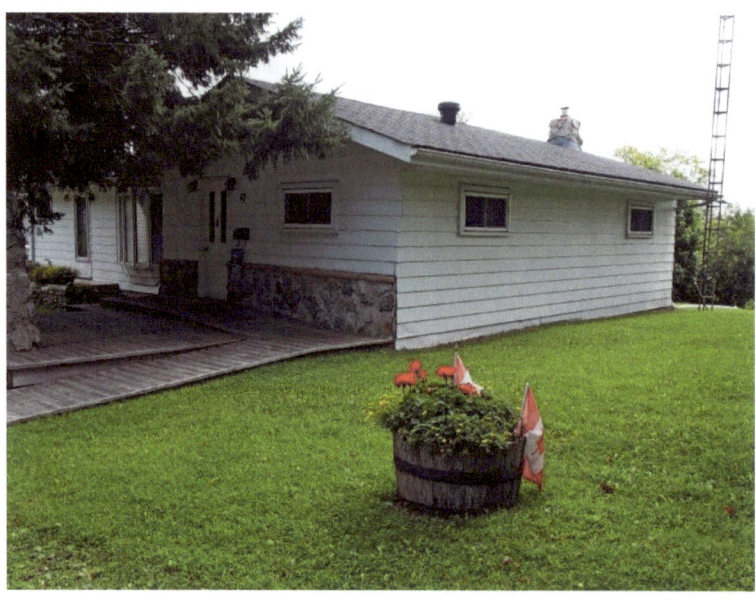

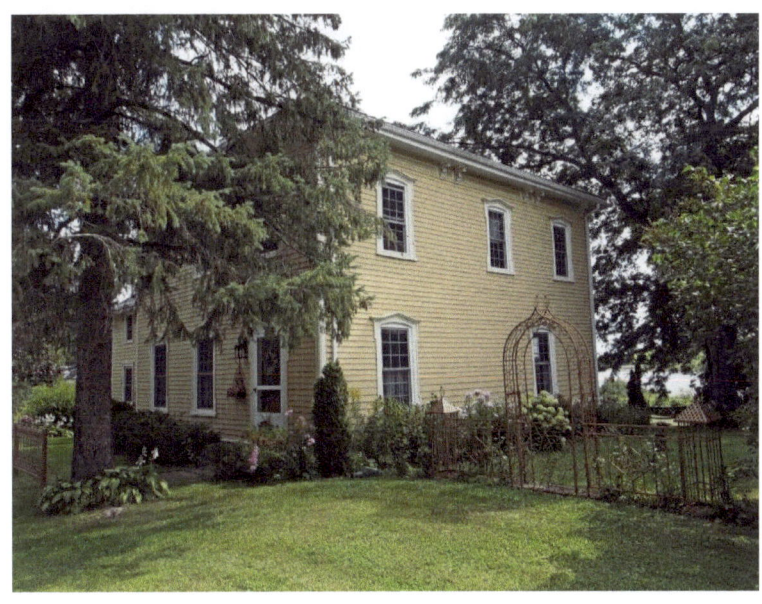

8 Mill Street – hip roof, paired cornice brackets, sash windows

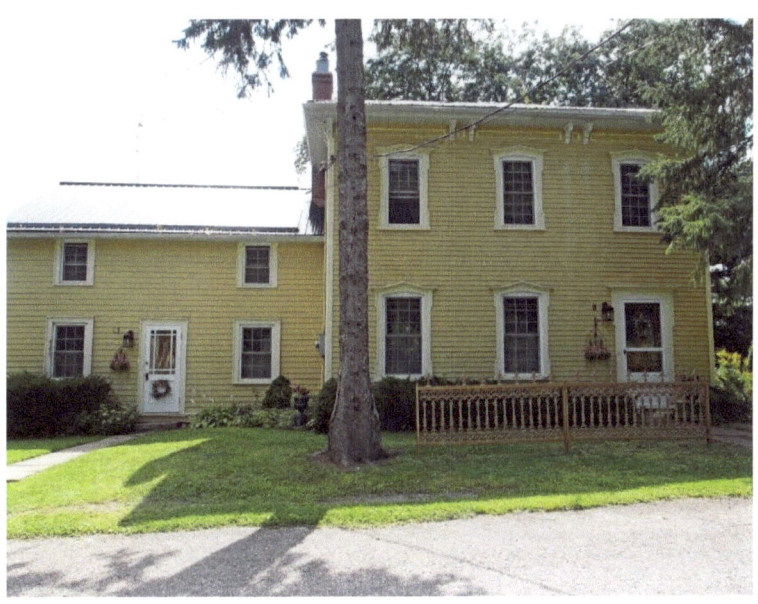

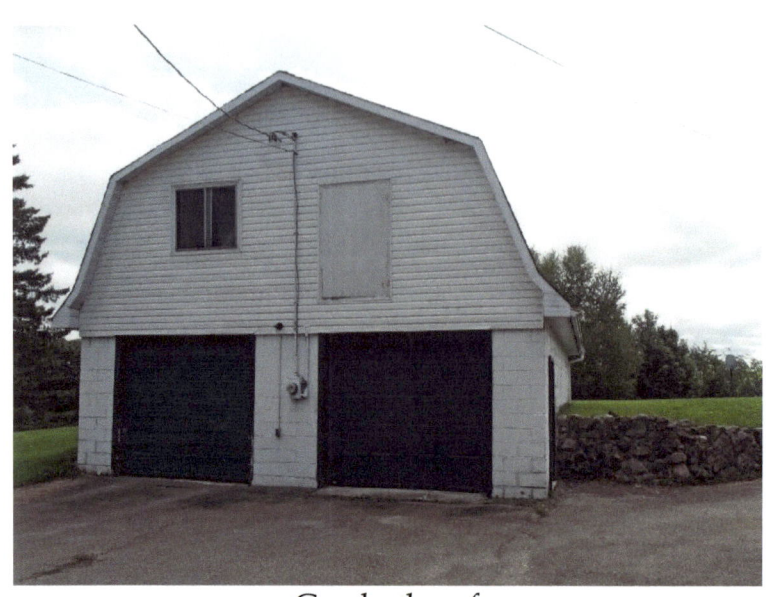

Gambrel roof

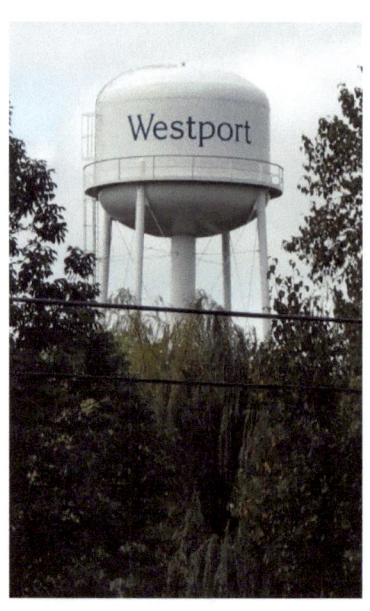

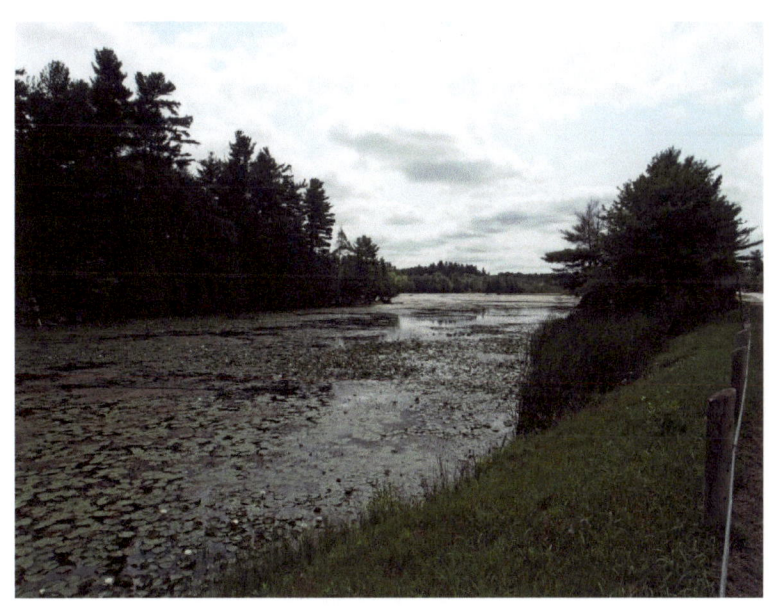

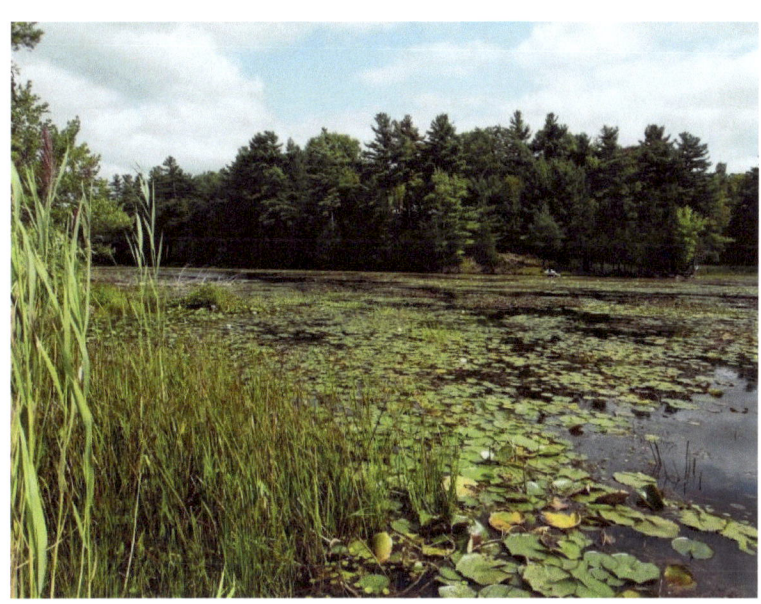

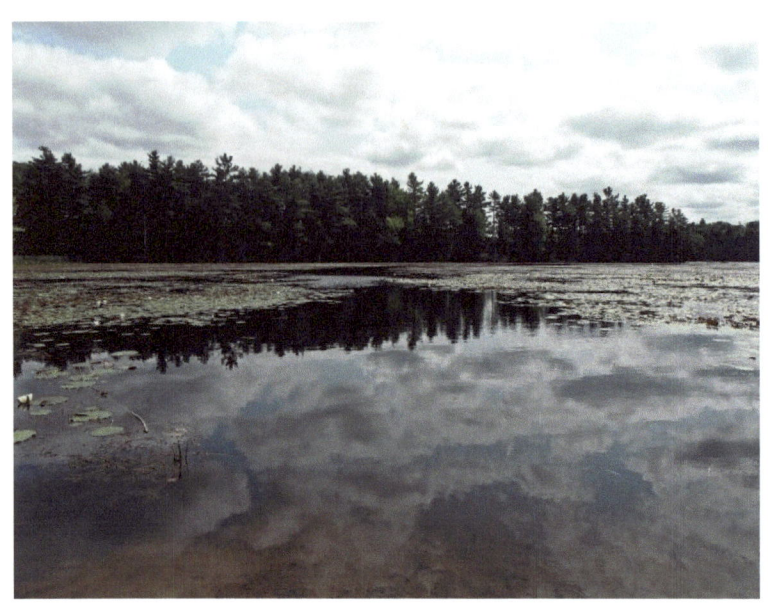

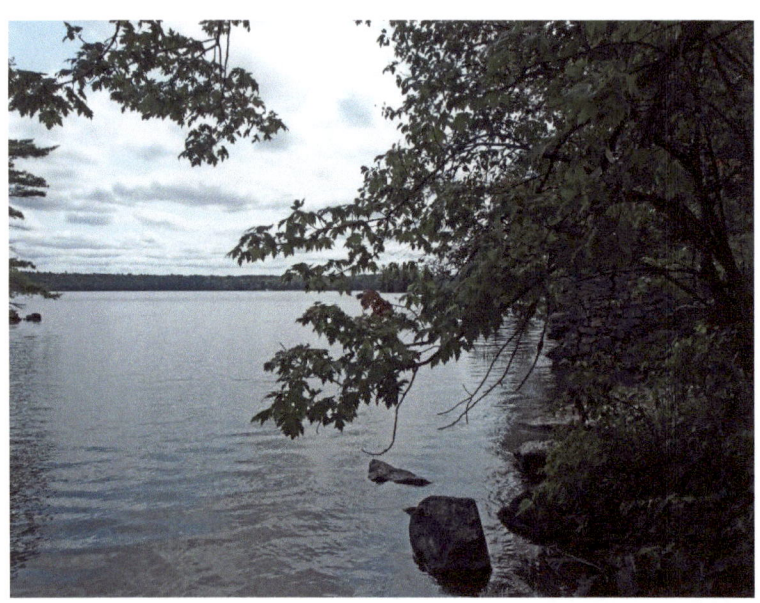

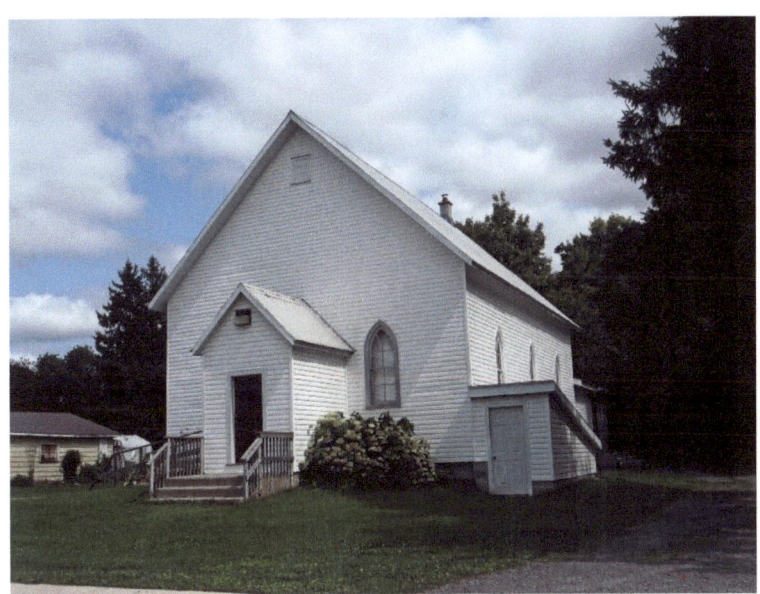

Perth Road United Church, Perth Road Village

Perth Road Village and area existed as far back as 1792. The Perth Road (County Road 10) had come as far as Loughborough Lake in 1864; it was finished in 1874 as a main artery linking Cottage Country to the city of Kingston as well as Westport and Perth. James Stoness and his wife Mary (Buck) operated the Post Office on the east side of Perth Road. Mary did some dressmaking. The village was called Stoness Corners for a time in history because there was a Stoness on each side of the road. There were many businesses in Perth Road - blacksmith shops, five or more stores, a cheese factory, garage and service station where gas was sold, sawmills, a mica shop, a seamstress and dressmaker. There were many churches, one room schools, a post office and a doctor's office. The mines in the area brought many more settlers.

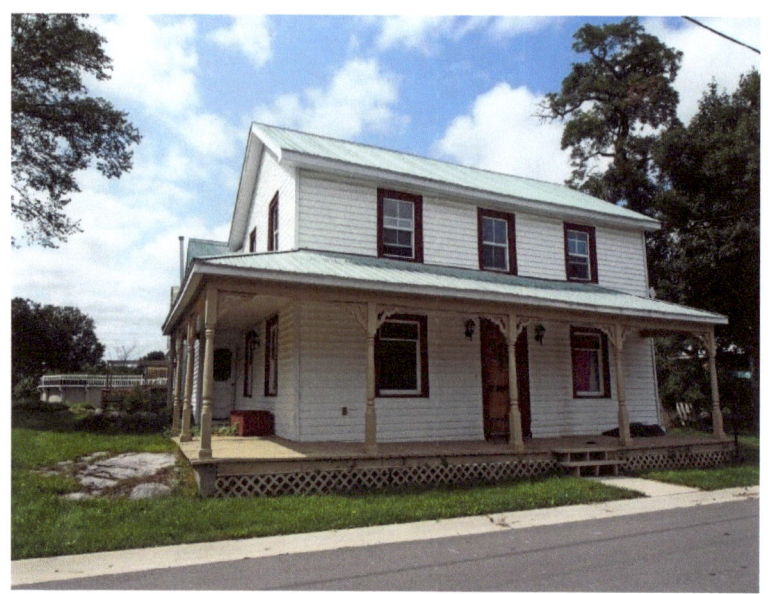

Bric-a-brac on porch pillars

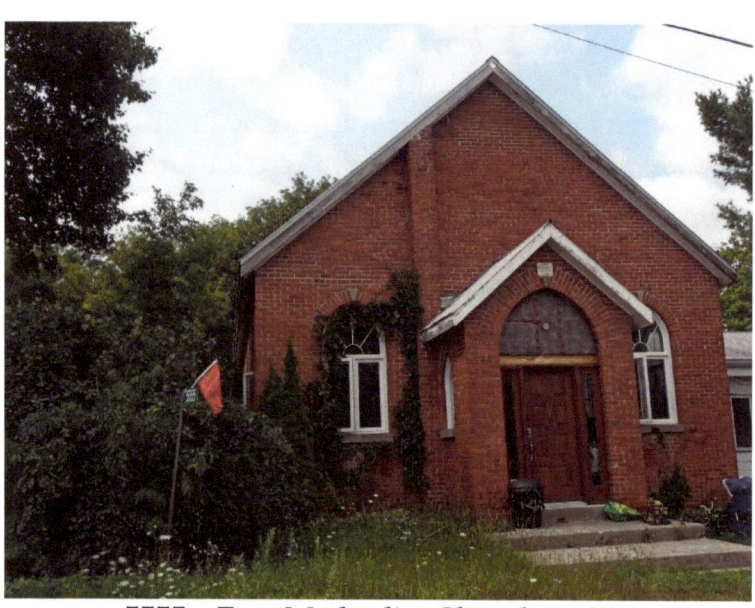

5555 – Free Methodist Church – 1944

Inverary

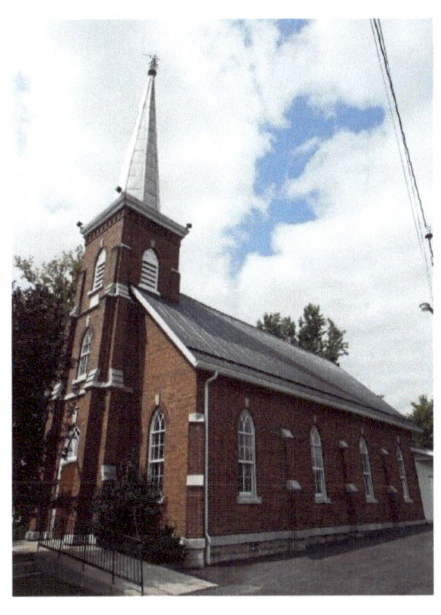

Inverary United Church (Methodist Church 1877) – Gothic
Revival – lancet windows, buttresses

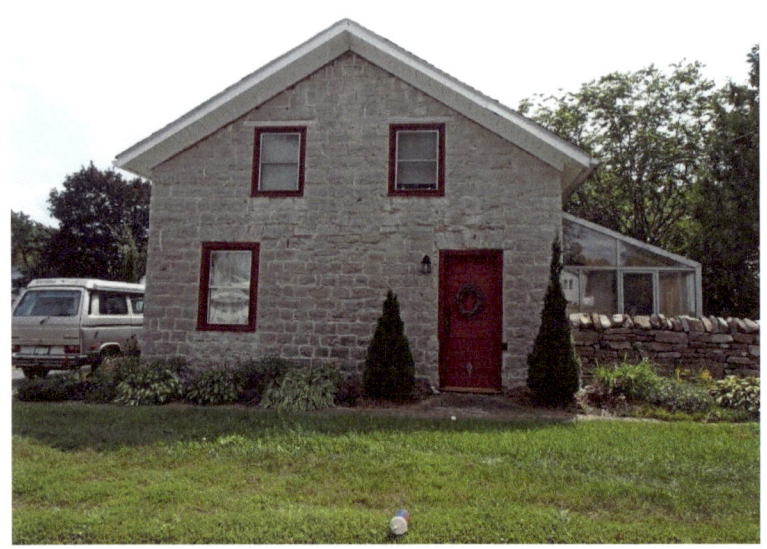

Inverary

Elginburg

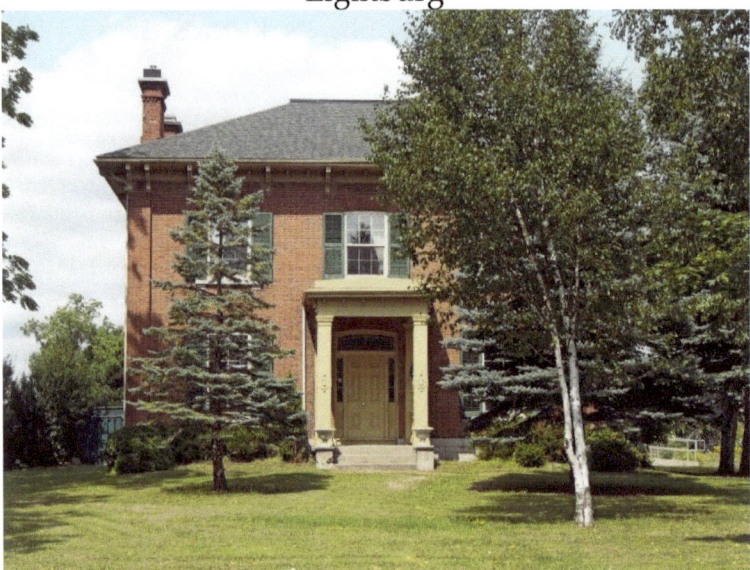

Hip roof, cornice brackets

Port Elmsley

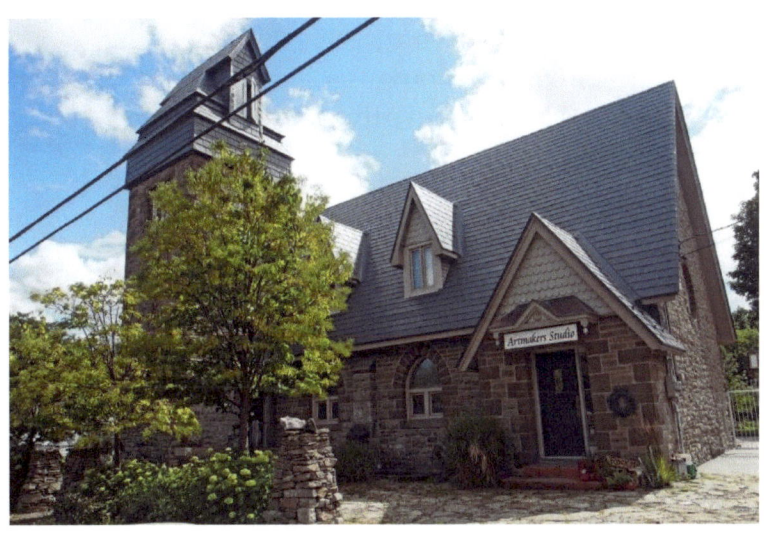

Stone buildings

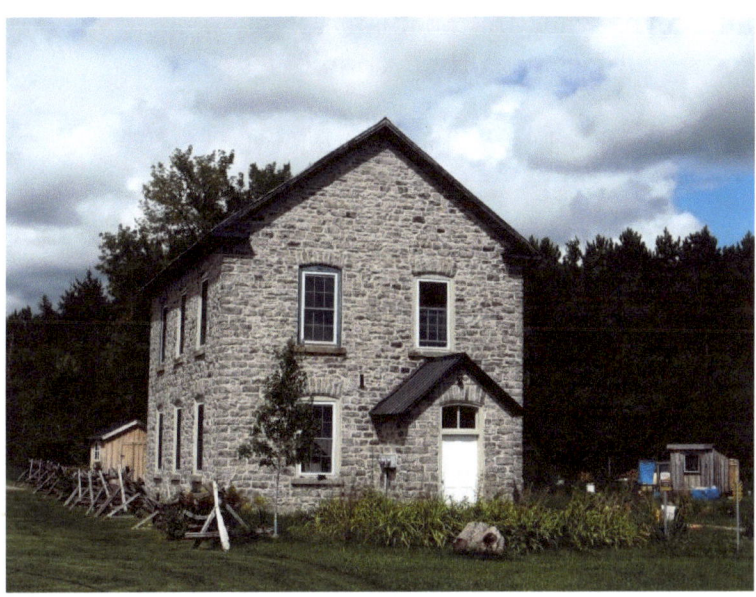

Cornice return on gable

Bay Window: A window that projects out from a wall, in a semicircular, rectangular, or polygonal design. Used frequently in Gothic and Victorian designs. Example: Page 19, Westport	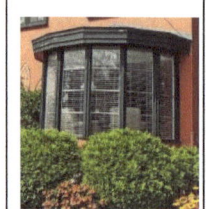
Brackets: a decorative or weight-bearing structural element which forms a right angle with one side against a wall and the other under a projecting surface such as an eave or roof. Example: 8 Mill Street, Page 35, Westport	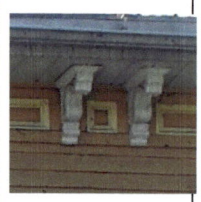
Buttress: a masonry structure built against or projecting from a wall which serves to support or reinforce the wall. In Canadian architecture, they are sometimes used for decoration. Example: Inverary United Church, Page 41	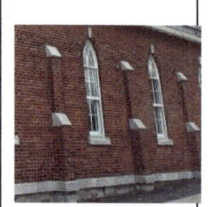
Capital: The uppermost finish or decoration on a column. An Ionic column has a small base, a thin elegant shaft, and a capital composed of volutes which are carved whirls or twists that take the form of a scroll. Example: 11 Church Street, Page 28, Westport A Doric column is characterized by a plain column with no base, a shaft with twenty flutings, and a simple capital with a simple Example: Page 10, Westport	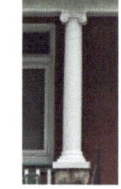 Ionic 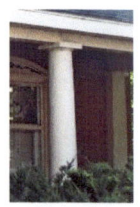 Doric

Cobblestone architecture: Refers to the use of cobblestones embedded in mortar as a method for erecting walls on houses and commercial buildings. Example: Page 20, Westport	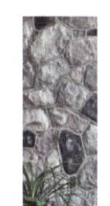
Cornice Return: decorative element on the end of a gable. Example: Port Elmsley, Page 43	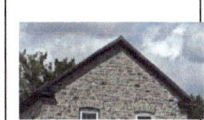
Dichromatic brickwork: the use of two colours of brick, tile or slate to decorate a façade. Example: 25 Bedford Street, Page 14, Westport	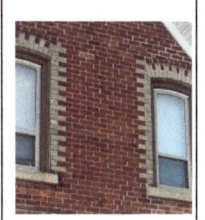
Dormer: (French for "sleep") a gable end window that pierces through the plane of a sloping roof surface to create usable space in the top floor or attic of a building by adding headroom. Example: Page 5, Westport	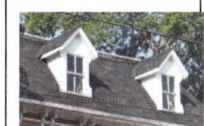
Gable: the triangular portion of a wall between the edges of a sloping roof. Example: 33 Main Street, Page 11, Westport	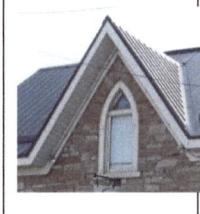

Gambrel Roof: a symmetrical two-sided roof with two slopes on each side; the upper slope is positioned at a shallow angle, while the lower slope is steep. It is similar to a mansard roof, but a gambrel has vertical gable ends instead of being hipped at the four corners of the building. Example: Page 36, Westport	
Hipped Roof: a roof where all sides slope downwards to the walls with no gables. Example: 11 Church Street, Page 28, Westport	
Keystones and Voussoirs: a voussoir is a wedge-shaped element used in building an arch. A keystone is the central stone that locks all the stones into position, allowing the arch to bear weight. A keystone is often enlarged and embellished. Example: Page 5, Westport	
Lancet Window: a tall, narrow window with a pointed arch at its top. Example: Inverary United Church, Page 41	

Mansard Roof: This style was popularized by Francois Mansart (1598-1666), an accomplished architect of the French Baroque period and especially fashionable during the Second French Empire (1852-1870). This roof is almost flat on the top section, with two slopes on each of its sides with the lower slope at a steeper angle than the upper and having dormer windows. Example: Page 5, Westport	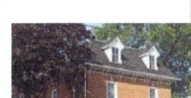
Pediment: a triangular section above the door or portico, usually supported by columns. The inside of the triangle is called the tympanum. Example: Page 6, Westport	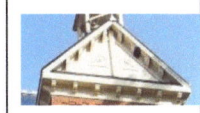
Quoin: masonry blocks at the corner of a wall, often a decorative feature, usually larger or of a different colour than the rest of the wall. Example: 27 Bedford Street, Westport, Page 15	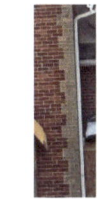
Tower: A circular, square, or octagonal vertical structure higher than the surrounding structure that is usually part of an existing building and is created either for extra defense or for a specific purpose such as a clock or a bell tower. Example: Page 10, Westport	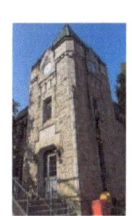

Transom Window: the light above the doorway, also called a fanlight. Example: Page 5, Westport	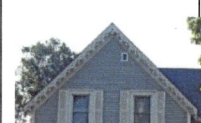
Verge board and Finial: also called bargeboards – hang from the projecting end of a roof and are often elaborately carved and ornamented. **Finial:** ornament added to the top of a gable, pinnacle, canopy or spire – a Gothic element. Example: Page 7, Westport	

Château, 1880–1930 **-** The Château Style is a grand adaptation of the sixteenth-century French chateaux of the Loire Valley. The fortified castles of medieval France were translated in Ontario into asymmetrical, irregular and equally elegant hotels, convents, and imposing private houses for the wealthy. The bases of this style are steeply pitched roofs with plenty of dormers, turrets, gables, conical towers, lunettes, and iron cresting. Ornamentation is lavish with intricate string courses, corbel tables, finials and crockets. The walls are generally finished stone or stucco and the roofs, especially on commercial buildings, are often copper left to develop a patina of soft green. Château style can be distinguished from Italian Villa and Queen Anne Revival by the roof line and pitch. Example: Westport Post Office, Page 10	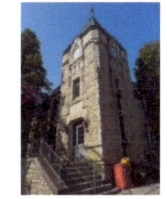
Gothic Revival, 1830-1890 – These decorative buildings have sharply-pitched gables with highly detailed verge boards, pointed-arch window openings, and dichromatic brickwork. It is a common style in Ontario. Example: 25 Spring Street, Westport, Page 27	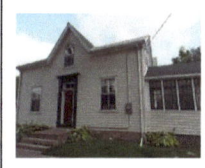

Italianate, 1850-1900 – A two story rectangular building with a mild hip roof, a projecting frontispiece, and generous eaves with ornate cornice brackets was the basis of the style; often there are large sash windows, quoins, ornate detailing on the windows, belvederes and wraparound verandahs. Italianate commercial buildings often have cast iron cresting and elegant window surrounds. Example: 11 Church Street, Westport, Page 28	
Second Empire, 1860-1880 – The mansard roof is the most noteworthy feature of this style and is evidence of the French origins. Projecting central towers and one or two-storey bays can also be present. Example: Page 5, Westport	
Victorian - In Ontario, a Victorian style building can be seen as any building built between 1840 and 1900 that doesn't fit into any of the other categories. It encompasses a large group of buildings constructed in brick, stone, and timber, using an eclectic mixture of Classical and Gothic motifs. Example: 25 Bedford Street, Westport, Page 14	

www.ingramcontent.com/pod-product-compliance
Lightning Source LLC
Chambersburg PA
CBHW040921180526
45159CB00002BA/563